returnblessings

a WATER book

water

Women's Alliance for Theology, Ethics and Ritual

returnblessings

ECOFEMINIST LITURGIES RENEWING THE EARTH

DIANN L. NEU

The Pilgrim Press
Cleveland

d e d i c a t i o n

to MARY E. HUNT with whom I return blessings

The Pilgrim Press, 700 Prospect Avenue, Cleveland, Ohio 44115-1100
pilgrimpress.com

© 2002 Diann L. Neu
All rights reserved. Published 2002

For additional assistance in constructing liturgies, contact WATER, the Women's Alliance for Theology, Ethics and Ritual, 8035 13th Street, Silver Spring, MD (phone 301-589-2509; fax 301-589-3150; e-mail water@hers.com)

Printed in the United States of America on acid-free paper

07   06   05   04   03   02   5   4   3   2   1

Library of Congress Cataloging-in-Publication Data
Neu, Diann L., 1948–
　　　Return blessings : ecofeminist liturgies reviewing the earth / Diann L. Neu.
　　　　　p.　cm.
　　　"A WATER book"—P.
　　　Includes bibliographical references (p.) and index.
　　　ISBN 0-8298-1486-8 (pbk.)
　　　1. Feminist theology.　2. Ecofeminism.　3. Liturgics.　I. Title: Return blessings.
　　II. Title.

BT83.55 .N48　2002
264'.0082—dc21

2002068436
CIP

contents

PREFACE

hese liturgies were created for
and with the feminist liturgy community of WATER, the Women's
Alliance for Theology, Ethics and Ritual; SAS (Sisters Against
Sexism), a women-church liturgical community in the Washington,
D.C., area; and various international feminist and justice gatherings.
They document women's Earth-centered prayer. They open up the
opportunity for mutuality and dialogue between nature and
women. They challenge the andocentric vision of Western religious
and patriarchal civilization that exploits the Earth, women, and all
powerless people. They sharpen individual and community awareness of the cyclical nature of life, remembering that all are creatures
of the sun, the moon, the tides, and the seasons.

These liturgies have been adapted and readapted by groups
worldwide. They invite you and your community to open your-
selves to the energies of the seasons in your region and to connect
with the cycles of life. They call feminists to do the work of creating and celebrating ecofeminist liturgies with our communities and
practicing their message: renew Earth.

I offer them as models for the ones that you and your community might celebrate. Adapt them to the needs of your community. You may need different readings, perhaps more scripture, or more reflections from your context or other cultures. Your community may have special songs they want to use; you may want more silence. Some in your group might want to write their own prayers and reflection, blessings and songs. The possibilities are endless.

I am very grateful to WATER for providing me for over twenty years a place to live out my call to do feminist liturgical ministry. The WATER community has been invaluable in this work. Mary Hunt shared her keen theological reflection and sharp analysis of the texts. Carol Scinto provided precise editing and renewing insights. Cindy Lapp offered suggestions for music and readings that were often just what was needed. Marge O'Gorman tracked down footnotes. Interns, visiting scholars, and international colleagues told me stories of the ecofeminist liturgies that they created and celebrated in their countries and cultural contexts. The WATER Alliance worldwide has been part of these liturgies.

Thank you to the staff at Pilgrim Press for bringing this book to final form, especially Timothy Staveteig, the publisher, and Kris Firth for editing every detail.

May these liturgies invite readers and participants to reclaim and redevelop values and ideologies that both celebrate and ensure a more balanced relationship with the environment upon which we depend. May they instill a sense of respect for creation as a source of life. May they invite us to perceive the environment both as a gift to be enjoyed by divine favor and as a responsibility to take care of, since ultimately it belongs to the Creator Spirit, Wisdom Sophia. May they lead us to develop a sense of gratitude and respect for nature. May they move us to alleviate some of the problems we face because of environmental crises and injustices. May they call us to return blessings so that all may live an abundant life.

one

AN ECOFEMINIST LITURGICAL VISION

I begin with memory and imagination. When asked to create an ecofeminist liturgy that would light the way into the next thousand years, the metaphor of *return blessings* captured my attention. I remembered that all creation holds blessings that are needed for life's cycles to continue from generation to generation. I imagined a universe where all living things depend on one another in the struggle of ecojustice for all. I prayed then and I pray now:

> Return blessings, O Holy Ones,
>> So life's cycles can continue with beauty, balance,
>>> and abundance.
>> May life's cycles return blessings.
>
> Return blessings, Sacred Earth,
>> So air, water, fire, and food can nourish all we hold dear.
>> May air, water, fire, and food return blessings.

1

Return blessings, Beloved Sisters and Brothers,
    So all creation can share pleasure and do justice.
    May all creation return blessings.

Return blessings, Crawling Creatures and Winged Friends,
    So the Earth can be renewed.
    May the Earth return blessings.

Return blessings, Trees, Flowers, Rivers, Mountains,
    So nature can refresh all spirits.
    May nature return blessings.

Return blessings, Stars, Moons, Planets, Galaxies,
    So wonder can nourish all visions.
    May wonder return blessings.

Return blessings, Changing Seasons,
    So life's cycles can continue in peace.
    May life's cycles return blessings.[1]

My earliest childhood memories are intertwined with these blessings of the cosmos. Growing up in Indiana on Lake Manitou, later Lake LaSalle, and then on the small lakes of St. Mary-of-the-Woods, I knew God first through the rhythms of the seasons. I cherished the return of spring when dogwood trees colored the woods with the beauty of their white and pink blossoms and thunderstorms electrified the skies. I longed for summer days when we lived on the spring-fed lake—swimming, boating, fishing, and playing. I gazed in wonder and awe at the autumn trees as their brilliant colorful images reflected in the water and fierce winds shook the leaves from their limbs. I rejoiced when winter snows transformed Earth into a wonderland for ice-skating, sledding, making snow angels, and huddling close to the fire as temperatures fell.

Nature was my friend. Life, death, and rebirth were its lessons. I knew the trees by name and could forecast the weather by looking at the clouds. When I was ten years old, the whirling maple seeds fascinated me. I created a liturgy as I planted ten of them in our yard. These trees and I have grown up together. Walking with the diverse beauties and mysteries of the Earth and the stars, I realized early in life that I am never alone. Nature is always there, and may this ever be so. My world then was full of childhood wonder and awe. Contemplating this beauty, I found reserves of strength that have endured throughout my life. Nature taught me about the Divine and prayer. When a family pet died, I created a burial ceremony and invited my Catholic, Protestant, and Jewish friends to mourn with us. The cycles of the seasons taught me to treasure life's changes.

Today I interact with these blessings of the universe from my urban home in Silver Spring, Maryland. Each morning I begin my day with a liturgy of gratitude for being part of creation's web of relationships. I breathe with the world's breathing. I am present with the body of the world and with the bodies of those I love. I listen to the wind play the chimes on the porch and pay attention to the birds as they announce the return of spring and eat from the feeder that hangs from a one-hundred-year-old oak. I hear water flow through the fountain and watch the fish swim in the little pond on our deck. The squirrels run along the fence as I cook with the fresh herbs grown in the garden. I am thankful for these encounters. This passionate relationship with nature compels me to return blessings by creating ecofeminist liturgies to strengthen women and empower communities to restore our relationship with creation and resist violence against nature.

Despite this beauty, a quick glance at the daily newspaper or the evening news, a short walk into Washington, D.C., and I realize the need to connect liturgy with solidarity. I lament and grieve with women, children, and men worldwide because creation is being abused and violated daily. Ecological disasters that are human-made are destroying the cosmos. Global warming that threatens life for generations to come is killing parts of Earth. Toxic chemicals and pesticides that are dumped into lakes, rivers, and oceans are polluting the waters. Car and truck pollution is fouling the air. Nuclear fallout could damage the sun and the stars. In each instance of ecological fragility, women and children suffer the most because we are the most vulnerable.

Resisting this violence against creation, women all over the world are struggling for life. Feminists are calling for an "ecological ethic emphasizing the interconnectedness between humanity and nature."[2] We are making connections between ecology and our own lives. Grassroots movements of women are engaged in a practical ecofeminism around the globe. Women in the Chipko Andolan of India are hugging trees, defying the contractors' saws to prevent deforestation. Women of the Green Belt movement in Kenya are planting thousands of trees to halt desertification. Mothers in the Seikatsa Club in Japan are joining with farmers to obtain unpolluted food for their children. Women in Ireland are reclaiming Bridget's wells by cleaning them and reviving well rituals. Women of Greenham Common in the United Kingdom and women at the Trident base in Seattle, Washington, in the United States are camping around nuclear installations to stop war production. Women in Brazil are engaging in sustainable agriculture to feed their children. Women worldwide are demanding an end to violence against women: domestic violence, rape, prostitution, and economic injustice. Women worldwide are reviving women's spirituality.

These women see clearly that the survival of children, Earth, and ourselves is inextricably connected. They link the extreme threat to life on this planet and its repercussions for all descendents. They know the web of life on Earth is threatened by global warming and nuclear waste; dwindling forests and a weakened ozone layer; the phenomenon of climate change; pollution and toxic waste; cancer alleys created by chemical companies and refineries; birth defects and lead poisoning; deforestation and soil erosion; radioactive fallout and toxic contamination of sea, soil, and air; and alienation from nature in all forms.

For many, these actions of resistance are political, spiritual, and liturgical. Listening to these moving stories and standing in solidarity with women struggling for ecojustice, I have been reflecting on the question of how feminist liturgies might celebrate the blessings of creation and resist violence against nature. How might ecofeminist liturgies strengthen women spiritually and empower communities to engage in political action to save the Earth?

Since cofounding WATER, the Women's Alliance for Theology, Ethics and Ritual, in 1983, I have been invited by a variety of communities in many places and countries to create feminist liturgies with them. As we design liturgies from an ecofeminist perspective, I am mindful of the passion, pain, and wonder of creation. For many people, the heart of the spiritual life is found in rites and ceremonies, liturgies and rituals. Symbols such as water, bread, and candles combined with experiences of community, sacrament, and solidarity may reach an emotional, unconscious center in ways that little else does. For feminists, kyriarchal[3] liturgies are suspect and alienating because they have helped provide justification for the oppression of women and nature. Ecofeminist liturgies are designed to reconnect participants with nature, women, and the divine. They invite participants to feel the depth and sacredness of this relationship.

This book has emerged from liturgies that I have created over the past twenty years with WATER, the women-church movement of a "discipleship of equals," and communities of peace and justice. I took notice that I had been asked to design and celebrate many liturgies that focus on the Earth and its seasons. Since creating them, I have been reflecting on the question of how to share these gifts so that other feminist and justice communities can learn to create ecofeminist liturgies. What liturgical models can help communities imagine and reclaim Earth-connected worship? I began by asking metaphorically about returning blessings.

A look at the Table of Contents makes it clear that I have ordered the liturgies around the seasons. The cycle of the seasons repeats itself yearly and returns blessings as it moves from spring to summer to autumn to winter and back to spring again. This Wheel of the Year is the cycle of life—beginning, blossoming, coming to fruition, fading, dying and being reborn again.

Return blessings is a metaphor that expresses a vision of ecofeminist liturgies of struggle and transformation that actualizes the renewing presence of the Creator Spirit, Wisdom Sophia. To return blessings is to give thanks for what one has received. People of many religious traditions say grace before and after meals as a way of saying thank you to God, Allah, Yahweh, Sophia, the Holy One, for daily food. To return blessings is to provide a challenge for each creature to respect the sacredness of nature and to give back to creation in some way what we have taken so that the cosmic web of relationships can stay in balance.

In Hebrew scriptures, blessing, or *berakah,* is associated with the internal and external power of the soul. The one that is blessed is given the power to bless in return. In Sophia-logy, blessing is understood as bringing life and well-being to a household. Sophia returns her blessing of hospitality and table by inviting people to her home.

Come eat my bread,
Drink from my source,
Take shelter in my wisdom,
Be transformed by my fire
And dance with the rhythm of the universe.
Blessed are you among women.[4]

Janet Walton, U.S. Catholic feminist liturgist, writes: "Seen from a feminist perspective, blessing is a collaborative experience. Blessing is given and received simultaneously."[5] Letty Russell, U.S.

Presbyterian feminist theologian, extends this feminist vision to all creation: "blessing is seen as God's intention for full humanity of women together with men and for the mending of all creation. The blessing of Sarah and Abraham is understood as a gift of full personal, social, and ecological well-being, not only for the people of faith but for all of the groaning creation (Rom. 8:22–23)."[6]

Return Blessings is intended to bring life and well-being to the household of creation. The ecofeminist liturgies in this book restore covenanted relationships between all created life and ourselves; they renew connections between all living things and the active presence of Creator Spirit, Wisdom Sophia. They call communities to gather as "the body of God," a model that unites everyone and everything on the planet in relationships of interdependence.[7] They tell stories that deepen the bonds of kinship with the web of life. They engage participants politically to analyze the ecological crisis and resist participating in ecological destruction. They challenge people to question biblical and church traditions that oppress nature and women. They empower women, men, and children to imagine a world that returns blessings. They offer hope to a ravaged Earth and to those yearning for a renewed relationship with the universe and with the divine.

These ecofeminist liturgies call those who want to heal the world and renew the Earth to build strong liturgical communities of celebration and resistance. They nurture and symbolize new Earth consciousness. They invite us to breathe again, notice again, and feel again through personal and communal Earth prayers. They challenge us to take time to be with nature: sit under trees, walk by the sea, gaze at the stars, notice the crocuses, get back in touch with the living Earth. They call us to mourn the violation of nature and to midwife its healing and new birth. They challenge us to take ecofeminist liturgies to the streets in protest marches and demonstrations in order to transform consciousness about the ecological crisis. They reveal a feminist analysis that reflects how women, children, and men can heal creation by resisting the exploitation and subjugation of women and the Earth. As I reflect on feminist ecological insights, I ask how these insights can inform ecofeminist liturgies. What wisdom can ecofeminists share with feminist spiritual communities of struggle like WATER, Women-Church, the Re-Imagining Community, and peace and justice groups? How do feminists invite liturgical communities to return blessings so that women and Earth may heal and survive?

WOMEN HEALING CREATION: FEMINIST CHALLENGES

Feminists worldwide have explored the interconnection between ecology and feminism and have linked the domination of women and the abuse of the environment. They provide a feminist analysis that gives content to ecofeminist liturgies. Their writings have informed my ecofeminist liturgical vision. I name some of them here, using the voices of the authors, so that you can receive the challenges and blessings of ecofeminism in women's own words.

French feminist Francoise d'Eaubonne coined the term *ecofeminism* in 1972. She envisioned a planet that was "green again for all" and argued that only women could bring about such an ecological revolution.[8] Early writings by U.S. feminist theorists Susan Griffin in *Woman and Nature*[9] and Carolyn Merchant in *The Death of Nature*[10] identify the twin dominations of women and nature with the profit motive inherent in male power in Western culture. Griffin writes in her Prologue of the many ways women and men interact with nature:

He says that woman speaks with nature. That she hears voices from under the earth. That wind blows in her ears and trees whisper to her. That the dead sing through her mouth and the cries of infants are clear to her. But for him this dialogue is over. He says he is not part of this world, that he was set on this world as a stranger. He sets himself apart from woman and nature.

And so it is Goldilocks who goes to the home of the
three bears, Little Red Riding Hood who converses with
the wolf, Dorothy who befriends a lion, Snow White who
talks to the birds, Cinderella with mice as her allies, the
Mermaid who is half fish, Thumbelina courted by a mole.
*(And when we hear in the Navaho chant of the mountain that a
grown man sits and smokes with bears and follows directions
given to him by squirrels, we are surprised. We had thought only
little girls spoke to animals.)*

*We are the bird's eggs. Bird's eggs, flowers, butterflies, rabbits,
cows, sheep; we are caterpillars; we are leaves of ivy and sprigs of
wallflower. We are women. We rise from the wave. We are
gazelle and doe, elephant and whale, lilies and roses and peach,
we are air, we are flame, we are oyster and pearl, we are girls. We
are woman and nature. And he says he cannot hear us speak.*

But we hear.[11]

Vandana Shiva, environmental activist and theorist from India,
heard women speak and authored *Staying Alive: Women, Ecology and
Development*, the classic book about ecofeminism from the Two-
Thirds World. She lifts up a new insight about women and nature:

To say that women and nature are intimately associated is
not to say anything revolutionary. After all, it was pre-
cisely just such an assumption that allowed the domination of both women and nature. The new insight provided by rural women in the Third World is that women
and nature are associated, not in passivity but in creativity and in the maintenance of life.[12]

She goes on to speak about women's power to protect nature:

Women, as victims of the violence of patriarchal forms of
development, have risen against it to protect nature and
preserve their survival and sustenance. They have been in

the forefront of ecological struggles to conserve forests, land and water. They have challenged the Western concept of nature as an object of exploitation and have protected her, the living force that supports life. They have challenged the Western concept of economics and production of profits and capital accumulation with their own concept of economics as production of sustenance and needs satisfaction.[13]

Feminist theologians have raised the problem of identifying women with nature. They have challenged the role of religion in perpetuating the hierarchy of human over nonhuman and the right of the human to treat the nonhuman as private property—resources to be exploited. Feminist theologians from the West question social structures based on race, class, and gender. Feminist theologians from the Two-Thirds World and womanist theologians from the United States connect colonialism with the impoverishment of women and the impoverishment of the land. Coming from unique cultural contexts, women are working together to create a sustainable future for all creation.

Much work has been done in the areas of critique and reconstruction related to ecology, feminism, and theology. Rosemary Radford Ruether, U.S. feminist theologian, offers a metaphor in her early work *New Women, New Earth* that links closely the liberation of women from sexism with the renewal of creation.[14] In her later work, *Gaia and God,* she focuses on a harmonious union of women and nature. She writes: "an ecofeminist spirituality needs to be built on three premises: the transience of selves, the living interdependency of all things, and the value of the personal in communion."[15]

Rosa Dominga Trapasso, a Maryknoll Sister of the Talitha Cumi religious feminist group in Lima, Peru, speaks of the evolution to ecofeminism: "I dare to think that once the links between all forms of oppression and violence became clear, from oppression in the family to the destruction of the planet, feminism had to become ecofeminism."[16]

Sally McFague, U.S. feminist theologian, offers in *The Body of God* the model of the universe (world) as "God's body, a body enlivened and empowered by the divine spirit."[17] Later in *Life Abundant* she calls for an ecological reformation to replace the bankrupt and dangerous individualistic market model (in which each of us has the right to all we can get) that has failed us and is dangerous to the planet. The ecological model suggests a new vision of the abundant life for all.

> In this [ecological] story, human beings are not individuals with the power to use nature in whatever ways they wish. Rather, we are *dependent* on nature and *responsible* to it. In a sharp reversal, we do not control nature, but rely utterly on it. In this picture, human beings are products of nature and depend for our every breath and bite of food on it. We cannot live for more than a few minutes without air, a few days without water, a few weeks without food. The rest of nature does not, however, depend on us; in fact, if human beings were to disappear from the earth tomorrow, all plants and animals would be better off.[18]

She goes on to say the ecological model must be a shared life.

> We must envision models of abundant life based not on material goods, but on those things that really make people happy: the basic necessities of food, clothing, and shelter for themselves and their children; medical care and educational opportunities; loving relationships; meaningful work; an enriching imaginative and spiritual life; and time spent with friends and in the natural world. In order to move toward this good life, we will need to make changes

at every level: personal, professional, and public—how we live in our houses, how we conduct our work lives, and how we structure economic and political institutions.[19]

Carol Christ, a U.S. thealogian now living in Greece, suggests in her *Rebirth of the Goddess* that we overcome the dualistic splits of body/mind, culture/nature by practicing "embodied thinking" and by reminding ourselves that we are part of nature. She writes: "The image of the Goddess also evokes the sacredness of nature. This confirms a deep intuition that has been denied in our culture: that we are nature and that nature is body."[20]

Dolores Williams, U.S. womanist theologian, connects abuse of nature with racist violence against African American women during slavery in an essay, "Sin, Nature, and Black Women's Bodies." "Very few people made the connection between America's contribution to the abuse and exploitation of the natural environment today with the dominating culture's historic abuse and exploitation of African American women's bodies in the nineteenth century."[21]

She observes:

> Breaking the spirit of nature today through rape and violence done to the Earth, and breaking the spirit of nineteenth-century slave women through rape and violence, constitute crimes against nature and against the human spirit. Inasmuch as some Christianity has historically advocated that God gave man [sic] dominion over nature to use to his own advantage, it has not been difficult to create rationales to support this rape and violence. Christian slaveholders, believing they had ownership over the lower orders of nature (i.e., lower than themselves, who were the "highest" order of nature), assigned black men and women to the order of subhuman, on par with the lower animals. Thus these black people needed to be controlled.[22]

Teresia Hinga, a Kenyan theologian now living in the United States, argues that the current ecological crisis in Africa has more to do with the historical developments on the continent, particularly after nineteenth-century colonization.

> Not only did the colonizers disregard the values and environmental ethics of the people they conquered, they also superimposed their own view of the human relationship with nature. In Africa, the Christian ethic of domination, which is implicit in certain readings of the Genesis account of creation, supported well the imperial ideologies that propelled the colonialist project.[23] This combination allowed gross abuse of the environment at all levels.[24]

Ivone Gebara, a Brazilian feminist theologian and philosopher who lives and works in Recife, poses key questions about feminism and ecology in *Longing for Running Water*:

> The first questions we need to ask ourselves are, In what ways do the feminist and ecological issues change our understanding of our own reality? Are they merely new topics to be reflected on and integrated into our traditional ways of thinking, or will dealing with them lead us to work at modifying the very models we use to think about the world?[25]

As we change our understanding of reality, we begin to challenge language, church, and biblical and liturgical texts. Dr. Gebara reminds us: "The catechism's understanding of humanity is marked by an absolute *discontinuity* between the Creator God and all of creation."[26]

> The Christian tradition in which we have been educated has always insisted on opposing Earth to heaven. In the context of this opposition, it taught us to wish for

heaven—to dream of it and to think of ourselves first and foremost as citizens of heaven. The Earth is just one planet among many, a place we are merely passing through. We are all destined for heaven—the place in which God dwells, the place of all that is good, eternal, and beautiful . . . The story of our denial of Earth in favor of heaven is very old.[27]

Feminists, spiritual leaders, and feminist liturgists have been influenced by ecofeminism. They are creating Earth ceremonies, rituals, and liturgies, and they are beginning to write about them. Carol Lee Sanchez, teacher and poet, native New Mexican of Laguna Pueblo, Lakota, and Lebanese heritage, writes of the inspiration for creating Earth ceremonies:

Every ceremony and sacred rite ever practiced on this planet was invented by humans to be performed by humans—one or hundreds. The motivation is generally inspired by witnessing of the mysteries and cycles of transformation continuously assailing our physical senses. The awe we experience—the joy, love, or grief that overwhelms us—inspires us to express in some fashion our brief encounter with that which is beyond physical touch but is within reach of our inner senses. When this happens, we achieve a kind of "knowing" that we have somehow been touched by something beyond us. A knowing that we cannot articulate often leads us to celebrate this personal event (or in many cases, communal event) through some form of expression. When tribal peoples experienced a brief encounter with the Great Mystery, they celebrated this experience with chanting and rhythmic movements. The Tribes view these celebrations or ceremonies as sacred because the intent of the performers and the witness/participants is one of reverence and respect.[28]

Victoria Tauli-Corpuz, from the Igorot tribal community in the Philippines, describes nature and rituals from her culture in this way:

> Nature to the indigenous women and men is thought of in spiritual terms. In spite of the aggressive Christianization drive among the Igorots, the majority is still animist in orientation and practice. Nature spirits are revered, respected and feared. Rituals are done to thank or appease nature spirits and ancestors. . . . Rituals coincide with agricultural cycles and the life cycles. . . . A ritual must be done when people alter the earth's natural state. So when a rice paddy is carved out from the mountainside, or a *swidden* (field) is made, those responsible should do a ritual to ask the permission and blessing of the spirits of the land.[29]

Denise Ackerman and Tahira Joyner from South Africa speak about the importance of women's stories of environmental activism for Earth-healing ritual praxis.

> An ecofeminist practical theological approach draws on stories in shaping liturgies, in preaching and in ministering. Teaching children the gospel stories, for instance, takes on a new guise and a new urgency when they are told in the context of the sacredness of all creation and the need to respect and preserve it. Our songs, prayers, rituals, and symbols can become vehicles for affirming the sacredness of all creation. Ecological awareness and Earth-healing praxis must become so commonplace that they become integral to all our acts of private and public worship, as well as focal to our acts of justice and charity.[30]

Teresa Berger, feminist theologian and liturgical scholar from Germany living in the United States, writes in *Women's Ways of Worship*:

Most Feminist liturgies display a positive emphasis on creation far more intensely than does the traditional liturgy. Feminist liturgies emerged in a time of heightened awareness of ecological crisis, and, with the 1980s, the development of an Ecofeminist theology. Where Feminist liturgies are influenced by Ecofeminist theology, Earth and nature come to be seen and venerated as the very Body of God.[31]

Kwok Pui-lan, Chinese feminist theologian from Hong Kong living in the United States, offers a challenge to ecofeminist liturgists and liturgical communities: "White women's periodic rituals in honor of the Earth (however important as ways to value both women and nature) are not radical enough to meet what is needed unless they are joined with concrete social action."[32]

Marjorie Proctor-Smith, U.S. feminist liturgist, echoes this challenge in *Praying With Our Eyes Open*:

> The process of claiming the power to create new ways of praying is full of risks. The obvious risks are of being misunderstood and misinterpreted, of being attacked for heresy, of being further marginalized by those who desire to protect the status quo, of being rejected or dismissed as irrelevant. . . .
>
> But there are other, less obvious, risks as well. Privileged white women risk replicating in the process and content of prayer the classist and racist practices that benefit us. All women's groups run the risk of trading religious, social, and political transformation for our personal spiritual comfort.[33]

Andy Smith, a Cherokee member of Women of All Red Nations, urges feminists to respect the integrity of Native American peoples and their spirituality. In her landmark essay "For All Those Who Were Indian in a Former Life" she writes:

Some white women seemed determined *not* to look into their own cultures for sources of strength. This is puzzling, since pre-Christian European cultures are also earth based and contain many of the same elements that white women are ostensibly looking for in Native American cultures. This phenomenon leads me to suspect that there is a more insidious motive for latching onto Indian spirituality.

When white "feminists" see how white people have historically oppressed others and how they are coming very close to destroying the earth, they often want to disassociate themselves from their whiteness. They do this by opting to "become Indian." In this way, they can escape responsibility and accountability for white racism.[34]

Veronica Brady, an Australian scholar, sites another challenge, one that *The Earth Bible Series* confronts:

The challenge offered by the ecological crisis and by the accusation that the lack of care for the earth and its creatures—the arrogant assumption that they exist merely for us to use and exploit—can be traced back to the Bible and, in particular, to God's command to increase and multiply, 'fill the earth and subdue it; and have dominion over . . . every living thing' (Gen. 1.28). In this view, far from being the word of life, the Bible brings a word of death and has little or nothing positive to contribute to the struggle for Earth and for the future of humanity.[35]

Heather Eaton, feminist biblical scholar from Canada, echoes this thinking:

Since feminists are not able to incorporate an authoritative sacred canon into a feminist paradigm,[36] the same is likely to be true of ecofeminists. For ecofeminists, as long as the Bible is accorded authoritative status, we accord authoritative status to patriarchy. Patriarchy, as a cultural ideology and phenomenon, depends upon the dual dominations of women and nature/Earth. For ecofeminists, the choices are explicit: to accept the patriarchal Bible as sacred and authoritative and be content to expose its patriarchy, or expose its patriarchy and reject it as sacred and authoritative.[37] From an ecofeminist perspective, the Bible can be accepted only as contingent and provisional.[38]

Many feminists approach the Bible as "dangerous memory." Yet many claim Wisdom Sophia as their source of spiritual authority. Anne Primavesi, English theologian, notes in "Ecofeminism and Canon" in *From Apocalypse to Genesis*, "In company with the figure of Wisdom in the Jewish scriptures, women must again raise their voices to recount their role in the fashioning, in the sustaining of the world."[39] She argues for "the inclusion of feminine and natural imagery in the Christian tradition and for women's rights to participate in the making of that tradition."[40]

Paula Gunn Allen, a Native American of Laguna Pueblo and Sioux heritage, meditates poetically, expressing empathy with nature and friendship with Wisdom Sophia, the great tree of life.

Our planet, my beloved, is in crisis; this, of course, we all know. We, many of us, think that her crisis is caused by men, or White people, or capitalism, or industrialism, or loss of spiritual vision, or social turmoil, or war, or psychic disease. For the most part, we do not recognize that the reason for her state is that she is entering upon a great initiation—she is becoming someone else. Our planet, my darling, is gone coyote, *heyoka*, and it is our great honor to attend to her rites of passage. She is giving birth to her new consciousness of herself and her relationship to the other vast intelligences, other holy beings in her universe.

Her travail is not easy, and it occasions her intensity, her
conflict, her turmoil—the turmoil, conflict, and intensity
that human and other creaturely life mirror. And as she
moves, growing and learning ever closer to the sacred moment of her realization, her turmoil, intensity, agony, and
conflict increase. . . .

What can we do to be politically useful, spiritually
mature attendants in this great transformation we are
privileged to participate in? Find out by asking as many
trees as you meet how to be a tree. Our Mother, in her
form known as Sophia, was long ago said to be a tree, the
great tree of life: Listen to what they wrote down from the
song she gave them.

> I have grown tall as a cedar on Lebanon,
> As a cypress on Mount Hermon;
> I have grown tall as a palm in Engedi,
> As the rose bushes of Jericho;
> As a fine olive on the plain,
> As a lane tree I have grown tall.
> I have exhaled perfume like cinnamon and acacia;
> Like galbanum, onzcha and stacte,
> Like the smoke of incense in the tabernacle.
> I have spread my branches like a terebinth,
> And my branches are glorious and graceful.
> I am like a vine putting out graceful shoots,
> My blossoms bear the fruit of glory and wealth.
> Approach me, you who desire me,
> And take your fill of my fruits.[41]

When Alice Walker, African American novelist, coined the
term *womanist* in 1983 in *In Search of Our Mothers' Gardens*, she sug-
gested an ecological emphasis by describing a womanist as one
who "Loves the moon. *Loves* the Spirit. Loves love and food and

roundness. Loves struggle. *Loves* the Folk. Loves herself. *Regard-less.*"[42] Later, in *Temple of My Familiar,* she speaks about the beatitudes or helpings that are related to the Earth and all living things.

> Helped are those who love the Earth, their mother, and who willingly suffer that she may not die; in their grief over her pain they will weep rivers of blood, and in their joy in her lively response to love, they will converse with trees. . . .
>
> Helped are those who find the courage to do at least one small thing each day to help the existence of another—plant, animal, river, and human being. They shall be joined by a multitude of the timid.
>
> Helped are those who lose their fear of death; theirs is the power to envision the future in a blade of grass.
>
> Helped are those who love and actively support the diversity of life; they shall be secure in their differentness.
>
> Helped are those who know.[43]

These women "who know" talk from significantly different contexts about their stories and those of women from diverse cultures. Yet their shared concerns for the Earth and those of countless women worldwide evoke solidarity. From their experiences we learn that ecofeminism is resistance to the associated exploitation and subjugation of women and the Earth. It examines the roots of the ecological crisis and misogyny, and their intertwining. It resists all forms of oppression and domination of women and the Earth. It advocates a mutual paradigm shift: we listen to nature and nature listens to us.

These ecofeminists offer profound challenges to those who create and celebrate ceremonies, liturgies, worship services, and rituals. How can these insights, challenges, and mutual listenings be reflected in ecofeminist liturgy? How do women's ways of knowing shape ecofeminist liturgies?

A TRANSFORMING ECOFEMINIST LITURGICAL VISION

When I designed each liturgy in this book, I listened to the challenges of these feminists and others. To make and do ecofeminist liturgy is to remember and imagine, to resist and transform story and tradition in the collective identity of a community.[44] It is to remember the unity and interdependence of all creation. It is to imagine a cosmos that is interrelated. It is to resist patterns of domination of women and the Earth. It is to transform ourselves into new ways of acting so that the Earth will survive. Liturgical memory and imagination record from generation to generation who and what we honor, whose stories we tell, what values we reinforce, what meanings we express, what transitions we mark, and what social roles we are expected to play. Liturgies create boundaries that order and systematize every way in which human society, the natural environment, and unseen worlds intersect and come together.

Out of women's experiences of the interconnection of the impoverishment of the majority of people, particularly women and children, and the impoverishment of the land, and out of women's need for a spirituality that does justice, a new feminist spiritual paradigm is evolving that connects ecology, feminism, and liturgy. These ecofeminist liturgies hold as sacred the Earth and all the life that the universe nurtures. They value both women and the Earth, are concerned with relationships and healing, and reflect women as interconnected with nature. Ecofeminist liturgies challenge the androcentric vision of Western religious and patriarchal civilization that exploits the Earth, women, and all powerless people. They advocate liberating the planet and freeing all creation from the devastation of racism, colonialism, classism, gender privilege, and war. They perceive sacred power as originating and emanating from God, who is Creator Spirit.

Hildegard of Bingen, twelfth century abbess, artist, poet, theologian, healer, mystic, liturgist, and ecologist, wrote words more than nine hundred years ago that call us to an ecofeminist liturgical consciousness:

> Glance at the sun.
> See the moon and stars.
> Gaze at the beauty of earth's greenings.
> Now,
> think.
> What delight
> God gives
> to humankind
> with all these things.
> Humankind should ponder God . . .
> recognize God's wonders and signs. . . .
> The earth . . . is mother of all. . . .
> The earth should not be injured.
> The earth should not be destroyed.[45]

These ecofeminist liturgies play a vital, grassroots role in the emergence of creation-consciousness. They are designed to help us honor the Earth and feel our connection to it. They invite us to hear the voices of nature. They critique the assumptions of nature reflected in symbols and songs, stories and sermons.

Spiritually, these ecofeminist liturgies recapture and express women's religious wisdom about the interconnections of creation. They invite participants to pray and work for the healing of the Earth, the return of harmony and balance. They are Earth-based, Earth-respectful responses to patriarchal abuse and its environmental destruction. They model mutual interdependency that replaces the hierarchy of domination. They call to sustain rather than exploit or destroy life on the planet. They emphasize that one's fundamental duty is to respect all and harm none.

Politically, these ecofeminist liturgies challenge patriarchy at its core. Domination and destruction of the natural world are linked with domination and oppression of the poor, women, people of color, and other powerless people. In counterpoint, they uphold nondominating and life-affirming relationships. They encourage participants in political action and ecoresistance. They support ecofeminist activism. They provide lamentations for the dying parts of our world and encourage restitution for the damage caused.

Educationally, these ecofeminist liturgies guide participants to a shared commitment to actions and changes in lifestyle on behalf of the Earth and its inhabitants. They show person and nature as complementary. They reflect ecological ways of knowing nature, and speak of the interconnection of all creatures—womankind and mankind; four leggeds, wingeds, and crawlers; plants and seasons; planets and stars; wind, thunder, rain, rivers, lakes, streams; pebbles, rocks, mountains, trees; spirited and holy people; gods and goddesses; all the intelligences and all the beings.

SEVEN ECOFEMINIST LITURGICAL PRINCIPLES

Ecofeminist liturgies invite communities to listen to nature, to live in right relation with all creation, and to take up the cause of justice for the Earth. They offer new awarenesses of body, symbol, language, music, environment, the Divine, and creation consciousness. Liturgy planners need to think about how the liturgy will reflect these awarenesses. I offer the following seven principles of ecofeminist liturgies to help the planning process. They reflect the basic framework of the liturgies and their connection to ecofeminism. Seven is the number of completion; Creator Spirit rested on the seventh day.

1. Ecofeminist liturgies value women's bodies and nature as holy vehicles of divine revelation, and honor women and nature in all their diversity as imaging the divine and as enjoying divine activity.

Creator Spirit, Wisdom Sophia, reveals herself through the universe, Earth, and all its components. Bodies and nature are good and holy. The liturgist needs to ask: how does this liturgy celebrate the body and the Earth as the Body of God? How does it 'value the physical body, emotional responses, and empathetic connections with the Earth and nature? How are postures and gestures used to embody prayer?

For example, in the end-of-winter liturgy "Green Power Returns," the Invocation calls upon the Spirits of the East, South, West, and North to "Return ever-greening life to planet Earth." While listening to the prayer, participants are invited to face each direction, if comfortable and convenient.

Spirit of the East, Winds of the Air Cycle,
You breathe in oxygen to awaken each cell;
You breathe out carbon dioxide to the grasses.
Return ever-greening life to planet Earth.

Spirit of the South, Metabolism of the Fire Cycle,
You touch seeds with sun that fuels all life;
You embrace the world with energy.
Return ever-greening life to planet Earth.

Spirit of the West, Flow of the Water Cycle,
Blood, lymph, mucus, sweat, tears;
You make powerful rivers run.
Return ever-greening life to planet Earth.

Spirit of the North, Creation of the Earth Cycle,
You replace each cell in the human body every seven years,
You contain all nourishment, all verdancy,
    all germinating power.
Return ever-greening life to planet Earth.

2. Ecofeminist liturgies use symbols and stories, images and words, gestures and dances, along with a variety of art forms that reflect the interconnectedness of creation.

Symbols bring together different levels of reality and relate them in a way that creates a new conscious experience. They bring together the literal word or image that is conscious, the unconscious to which it points and makes present, and the particular cultural context that gives it its unique form. Symbols often support images, emotions, or meaning beyond what we can see; they always stand for more than the obvious and known meaning. The liturgist needs to meditate and interact with symbols until they reveal their meaning. The liturgist needs to ask: how are nature symbols used in this liturgy; for example, water, air, fire, earth, seeds, bulbs? Does use of the image foster mutuality and increase consciousness of nature, or reinforce domination and subordination? How does the symbol convey the relationship between humanity and nature? Does the symbol reveal the inherent value of nature?

For example, in the end-of-winter liturgy "All Shall Be Well Again," each participant is invited to take a flower bulb. The leader says:

> Hold your bulb and pray after me:
> Source of Life, One who brings forth crocuses and daffodils,
>   (Echo)
> Praise to you for blessing the Earth with beauty. (Echo)
> Renew us with flowing water (Echo)
> Singing birds and spring light. (Echo)
> All shall be well again. (Echo)
> All shall be well again. (Echo)
> All shall be well again. (Echo)
> Amen. Blessed be. Let it be so. (Echo)

3. Ecofeminist liturgies use language that reflects the inherent goodness of women and the Earth.

Language functions to free or oppress. The liturgist needs to ask: does the language in readings and songs, blessings and prayers, foster false ideas that the Creator breathed life into users and those who would be used; that some are valued and others expendable; that some are sacred and others profane? Are organic images used in blessings, prayers, and introductions? Is the language inclusive of all creation?

For example, in the Earth Day liturgy, "Think Green as Hope for Planet Earth," participants share "Blessing the Fruits of the Earth." The leader begins:

> Creation shares power by giving us daily food. (*The leader takes the basket of fruits, nuts, bread, juice, and wine.*) Extend your hands, palms up, and let us bless these fruits of the Earth together. Please pray after me.
>
> > Blessed are you, Source of Nourishment, (*Echo*)
> > For creating these fruits of the Earth (*Echo*)
> > And sharing manna with your people as they
> > wandered in the desert. (*Echo*)
> > Air, fire, water, earth, and spirit combined to make
> > this food. (*Echo*)
> > Numberless beings have died and labored that we
> > may eat. (*Echo*)
> > Nourish us with the power of creation that we may
> > nourish life. (*Echo*)
>
> (*The leader passes the basket around for all to take and eat.*)

4. Ecofeminist liturgies use music that identifies with the Earth community.

Music enhances the mood of the liturgy. We retain much more readily what we sing than what is read to us. The melody gets into our bodies and we almost become the song. Poetic images transform old concepts. The liturgist needs to ask: does the music reflect that mutuality replaces domination? Do the words and symbols convey a positive interconnection between humanity and nature?

For example, in the late-summer liturgy "A Garden of Abundance," Carolyn McDade's "Song of Community" uses the symbol of weaving to express community:

> We'll weave a love that greens sure as spring,
> Then deepens in summer to the fall autumn brings
> Resting still in winter to spiral again
> Together my friends we'll weave on, we'll weave on
>
> *Chorus:*
> A love that heals, friend, that bends, friend,
> That rising and turning then yields, friend,
> Like the mountain to rain or frost in the spring
> Or darkness that turns with the dawn.
> It's by turning, turning, turning, my friend,
> By turning that love moves on.
>
> We'll weave a love with roots growing deep
> And sap pushing branches to wake from their sleep
> Bearing leaves burnt amber with morning's full sweep
> Together, my friends, we'll weave on, we'll weave on.
>
> *(Chorus)*[46]

5. Ecofeminist liturgies are celebrated in environments that reflect the sacredness of the Earth.

Ecofeminist liturgies need to do what they say. Therefore, it is good practice to hold services outside when possible. Identify prominent landmarks that surround your neighborhood (not humanmade ones). Find out the native plant and creature life in your area; explore the ecological relationship between plants, animals, insects, birds, earth, water, air, and winds. The liturgist needs to ask: what space and ambience will enhance this liturgy? How will we honor this place? What does this environment communicate about the relationship between humans and nature?

Some examples will help. Plan a service in a park, on a mountaintop, at the ocean, inside a circle of stones. Create prayer gardens or labyrinths to connect prayer and nature. Walk, pray, and pick up trash. When using an inside space, invite nature to enliven the celebration. Bring live trees or plants into the setting to reflect the seasons: a flowering tree for spring, a tomato vine for summer, a red maple for autumn, an evergreen for winter; plant them as part of the service. For weddings, use birdseed instead of rice; use fabric aisle runners, not plastic. Around the outside liturgical space plant berries and trees that attract birds, and put water into birdbaths.

6. Ecofeminist liturgies image the Divine as the source of life that sustains all creation.

Images for Creator Spirit, Wisdom Sophia, Goddess/God, like language, are used to free or oppress. Scripture is rich with diverse images of the Divine. Some of the many examples include water (Gen. 1:2, John 4:14), rock (Isa. 26:4), rose and lily of the valley (Song of Songs 2:1), light (Ps. 27:1), the eagle (Deut. 32:11–12), breath (Gen. 2:7), mother hen (Matt. 23:37), bear (Hos. 13:8), Wisdom Sophia (Prov. 9:1–3). In this book of ecofeminist liturgies I use some of these images and others that emerge from the integrity of the liturgy—Wisdom Sophia, Creator Spirit, Great Goddess, Source of Life, Great Spirit, Beauty, Power, Energy, Creator of All Things Living, Spirit of Renewal, Living Water, Restoring Holy One, Holy Creator, Goddess of Fire, Sustainer of All, Sustenance of All Life, Lover of All, Source of Creation, Great Mother, Holy One of Our Ancestors. The liturgist needs to ask: how will we name the Divine in this liturgy? What blessing will be used?

For example, the Sending Forth blessing from the springtime World Water Day liturgy, "Water to Make All Things New," speaks of the Divine as Wisdom Sophia, the Source of Life, the Source of Healing, and the Source of Eternal Rest.

> May Wisdom Sophia, the Source of Life,
> Heal and renew all water supplies.
> May Wisdom Sophia, the Source of Healing,
> Send gentle rains upon dry lands.
> May Wisdom Sophia, the Source of Eternal Rest,
> Return all life peacefully to the sea.

7. Ecofeminist liturgies motivate participants to sustain a balanced and diverse Earth community, to resist its oppressors, and to lament the violence and abuse that has been done to it.

Prayer and spirituality must be lived. Ecofeminist liturgies invite participants to practice what they have celebrated together. The liturgist needs to ask: how does this liturgy challenge participants to develop creation consciousness and resist violence? How can it encourage people to recycle, raise small crops, generate energy from renewable sources, compost? Shape public policy by critiquing and challenging toxic waste management, nuclear waste disposal, strip mining, air pollution standards, land sale? How does it use prayers of refusal—lament, curse, exorcism—as a way of motivating participants to say no to the violence against creation?

For example, in the late-autumn liturgy "The Roaring of Creation as Cries for Ecojustice," the participants begin by walking and listening to the Earth. They hear two people proclaim a Litany for Ecojustice and are invited to respond with the words, "We must work for ecojustice."

> LEADER ONE: Because many refuse to acknowledge that
> the Earth is a living, interrelated system.
>
> RESPONSE: **We must work for ecojustice.**

LEADER TWO: Because too many people have degraded fertile Earth into landfills, forests into deserts, running rivers into silted floodplains.

RESPONSE: **We must work for ecojustice.**

LEADER ONE: Because grave assaults on the biosphere—acid rain, desertification, waste accumulation, overpopulation, ozone depletion—rob us all of our heritage.

RESPONSE: **We must work for ecojustice.**

LEADER TWO: Because governments and corporations play economic and environmental concerns off against each other.

RESPONSE: **We must work for ecojustice.**

LEADERS ONE AND TWO: Because each form of life is integrated with every other form of life, and because we have not rallied to Earth's defense.

RESPONSE: **We must work for ecojustice.**

Later in the liturgy participants are asked to reflect silently on the cries for ecojustice that we have heard:

> (*Pause*) How will I respond? What action will I take to restore the Earth to its dignity and help the planet survive? How do my daily habits affect the survival of life on planet Earth? How can I change my lifestyle so that it reflects and enables a sustainable future for all of us and all our relations? (*Pause*)
>
> Invite a word of commitment to emerge from within you. (*Pause*) Touch one of the elements—air, fire, water, earth—and speak aloud your word of commitment.

THE SEASONS RETURN BLESSINGS

This ecofeminist liturgical vision is foundational to *Return Blessings*. When I designed each liturgy in this book, this vision was my guide. I organized the book around the seasons because all creation is affected by the changing relationships between the sun and the Earth. As Rachel Carson, U.S. scientist and writer, says simply and profoundly in *The Sense of Wonder:* "There is something infinitely healing in the repeated refrains of nature—the assurance that dawn comes after night and spring after the winter."[47]

In ancient times festivals and celebrations were firmly rooted in seasonal cycles. Today many holidays have their origins in the changing of the seasons. Not every part of the world has the same seasons, but each has its own rhythms. By returning to Earth liturgies, we can reconnect with the web of life. By celebrating ecofeminist liturgies we can enjoy lasting pleasures from contact with the earth, sea, and sky and we can resist the violence done to them.

The seasons return blessings from year to year. The ebb and flow from light to dark, winter to summer, sunrise to sunset is a metaphor for all life. The seasons reveal the rhythm of the universe and mirror the cycles of women's lives. They symbolize heightened moments of awareness and assure that everything passes and changes. Spring reflects childhood and puberty; summer connotes maiden and mother; autumn relates to menopause and wise woman crone; winter heralds death and rebirth to a new spring.

Seasonal festivals express and reveal the power of the Earth and the power of women. They are meeting grounds for the seasonal, celestial, communal, and personal aspects of living. Communities dance, sing, feast, fast, and dramatize important moments in the life of the universe and in our own lives. Through the seasons we connect with inner and outer cycles. Each season has its beauty and pain, death and resurrection. Each is connected with what went before and what will come after. The present links with the past and the future.

Seasons are interconnected and cannot exist without one another. Without spring there is no summer; lacking summer, no autumn; without autumn, no winter; and if winter never came, there could be no new spring. When we celebrate ecofeminist liturgies that honor the seasons, we acknowledge our interconnection with the Earth and the universe. Being linked with Earth's cycles is vitally important for the health and well-being of all creation. A first step is becoming more aware of the natural seasons. By witnessing the seasons and celebrating them in liturgies, we can develop a deeper connection between the Earth and ourselves. As we become more in tune with natural energy shifts, our lives become more balanced and are in harmony with the environment and with the divine.

THIS BOOK: *Return Blessings*

The ecofeminist liturgies in this book mark the turning points in the yearly Western calendar. Using the framework of the four seasons, I present four liturgies within each season and describe their liturgical texts. Be mindful that the northern and southern hemispheres celebrate opposite seasons, and in some countries there are fewer than four seasons. Be sure to adapt the texts to your own culture.

Part One, "Spring—Returning to Life," calls forth new life and renewal within participants and all creation. The liturgy "Welcome Spring Renewal" greets spring, approximately March 21 in the northern hemisphere (September 21 in the southern), the time of renewal and promise of new life, rebirth, and new beginnings. It reflects on how we experience the Divine, Creator Spirit, Wisdom Sophia, in spring. It calls forth sharing and action about personal and global qualities that need to be brought into harmony.

"Water to Make All Things New" celebrates World Water Day, March 22. It invites participants to connect with water, listen to its sounds, pray for a healing of the waters, and bless their bodies with this life-giving element.

"Think Green as Hope for Planet Earth" honors Earth Day, April 22. It invites participants to experience an interconnection with the pain and power of creation. It challenges all to think "green" and live an ecologically sensitive lifestyle to help the planet survive.

"Walk in Beauty" praises the beauty of the Earth in mid-spring, May (November). It invites participants to walk in beauty and restore beauty to the Earth so that it can be beautiful beyond seven generations.

Part Two, "Summer—Energized by the Sun," honors the healing energy that flows from the golden light and flaming sun. "Summer Solstice as Praise the Sun" celebrates the sun at its peak of solar power, around June 21 (December 21), and renews the community's ties to the Earth. It invites participants to feel the rainbow of colors from the sun, to share the fulfillment, passion, and creativity they wish for themselves and for the Earth.

The "Prayer of Directions" invites participants to face the directions of the universe: north, east, south, west, above, below, and center, and join in prayerful presence with creation that dwells there.

"A Garden of Abundance" celebrates the first harvest of the year in August (February), when fruits and vegetables are plentiful. It focuses on the abundance of the garden, the awareness of life's richness. It invites participants to notice areas of plenty in their lives and reflect on the harvest they will store up for the winter.

"The Earth Is Sacred" begins by inviting participants to acknowledge that "we have forgotten who we are." To reconnect with the Earth, the gathered lie down under a tree for a guided meditation. To show love and care for the Earth, they are invited to rid the world of destructive patterns, accept the rhythms of life and death, and become cocreators with Wisdom Sophia. They pull weeds, compost, and plant seedlings.

Part Three, "Autumn—Reaping the Harvest," opens participants to changes and transitions in life. "Deep Peace of the Changing Seasons" honors the autumn equinox, approximately September 21 (March 21), which balances the dark and the light, life and death, sleep and wakefulness. Once again night and day are of equal length. This liturgy focuses on spiritual change, inviting participants to describe connections to their religious past and spiritual future, and to give thanks for the insights they have received. To close, they connect with the deep peace of the running waves, the flowing air, the quiet Earth, and the shining stars.

"A Women's Harvest Festival" celebrates a harvest that is often overlooked, the contributions of women. This liturgy honors the ancestors who have passed on to us over the generations their wisdom and insights, their memories of the past and present. It honors women who have gone before us and made the world a more livable place for us and for the next generations. Participants are invited to weave their stories with those of biblical women, church mothers, goddesses, women of recorded history, the lost generations, grandmothers, and mothers.

"The Roaring of Creation as Cries for Ecojustice" invites participants to hear creation's lamentations and to take action to restore the Earth to its dignity. They begin by walking and listening to the Earth. Hearing cries for ecojustice, they declare, "We must work for ecojustice." They reflect on how their lifestyles affect the survival of planet Earth.

"Hallowed Be the Turning into Darkness" acknowledges the decline of light and the increase of darkness. This liturgy celebrates the closeness of the worlds of the living and dead. It invites participants to remember the dead, take a look at death, and focus on what is ending, dying, or needs to be changed in their own lives.

Part Four, "Winter—Renewing the Earth," honors the darkness. "Winter Solstice as from the Womb of Night" is the solar new year, on about December 21 (June 21). This winter solstice liturgy celebrates Chanukah, Kwanzaa, and Christmas. In it participants light and dedicate Chanukah candles to peace, Kwanzaa candles to the power of community and overcoming racism, and the Advent/Christmas candles to peace on Earth.

"Blessed Be the New Year" celebrates the season when spirits of hope and change intermingle. This divide between what has been and what is to come invites participants to contemplate new beginnings and articulate farewells. It invites the Great Spirit of Hope to bless this holy season.

"All Shall Be Well Again" invites participants to say goodbye to a difficult winter and welcome the renewal of spring. They light candles and ring bells to let the winter go. They plant bulbs and reflect on the springtime blooms for which they wish.

"Green Power Returns" celebrates the renewal of spring by honoring the Spirits of the east, south, west, and north for returning ever-greening life to planet Earth. It invites participants to renew the Earth by scattering grass seeds, reflecting on personal ever-greening life, and committing to an action to save planet Earth.

Return Blessings offers these ecofeminist liturgies to empower spiritual communities of struggle to be agents for sustaining the integrity of creation. These sixteen ecofeminist liturgies express women's religious wisdom about interconnection with creation. These liturgies challenge participants to mobilize communal resources for social change. They invite participants to restore the Earth to dignity by reconstructing Earth's body, the human body, and our relationship with all living bodies.

NOTES

1. I was invited to write this prayer for Elizabeth Roberts and Elias Amidon, eds., *Prayers for a Thousand Years* (San Francisco: HarperSanFrancisco, 1999), 204. It is central in the liturgy entitled *Return Blessings* that WATER gave to our donors at the beginning of this millennium.

2. Carolyn Merchant, *The Death of Nature: Women, Ecology and the Scientific Revolution* (New York: Harper & Row, 1980), xv.

3. Elisabeth Schussler Fiorenza, *Discipleship of Equals: A Critical Feminist Ekklesialogy of Liberation* (New York: Crossroad, 1983/1994), defines kyriarchy as hierarchical systems of domination that are church focused.

4. Proverbs 9:1–3, 5–6, adapted by Diann Neu.

5. Janet Walton, "Ecclesiastical and Feminist Blessing: Women as Objects and Subjects of the Power of Blessing," in Mary Collins and David Power, eds., *Blessing and Power* (Edinburgh, Scotland: T. and T. Clark, 1985), 78.

6. Letty Russell, *Church in the Round: Feminist Interpretation of the Church* (Louisville: Westminster John Knox Press, 1993), 117.

7. Sallie McFague speaks of the world or universe as God's body in her groundbreaking book *The Body of God: An Ecological Theology* (Minneapolis: Fortress Press, 1993).

8. Francoise d'Eaubonne, "Feminism or Death," in Elaine Marks and Isabelle de Courtivron, eds., *New French Feminists: An Anthology* (Amherst, MA: University of Massachusetts Press, 1980).

9. Susan Griffin, *Woman and Nature: The Roaring Inside Her* (New York: Harper & Row, 1978).

10. Merchant, *The Death of Nature*, xv.

11. Griffin, *Woman and Nature*, 1.

12. Vandana Shiva, "Let Us Survive: Women, Ecology and Development," in Rosemary Radford Reuther, ed., *Women Healing Earth: Third World Women on Ecology, Feminism and Religion* (Maryknoll, NY: Orbis Books, 1996), 70.

13. Ibid.

14. Rosemary Radford Ruether, *New Women, New Earth: Sexist Ideologies and Human Liberation* (New York: Seabury Press, 1975), 186–211.

15. Rosemary Radford Ruether, *Gaia and God: An Ecofeminist Theology of Earth Healing* (San Francisco: Harper & Row: 1992), 251.

16. Rosa Domingo Trapasso, "Ecofeminismo: revisando nuestra conexion con la naturaleza," *Con-spirando* 4 (June 1993), 3.

17. McFague, *The Body of God*, 142.

18. Sallie McFague, *Life Abundant: Rethinking Theology and Economy for a Planet in Peril* (Minneapolis: Fortress Press, 2001), 208.

19. Ibid., 209–10.

20. Carol Christ, *The Rebirth of the Goddess: Finding Meaning in Feminist Spirituality* (Reading, MA: Addison-Wesley, 1997), 8.

21. Delores Williams, "Sin, Nature, and Black Women's Bodies" in Carol Adams, ed., *Ecofeminism and the Sacred* (New York: Continuum, 1993), 24.

22. Ibid., 27–28.

23. See Genesis 1:26.

24. Teresia Hinga, "The Gikuyu Theology of Land and Environmental Justice," in Ruether, *Women Healing Earth*, 173.

25. Ivone Gebara, *Longing for Running Water: Ecofeminism and Liberation* (Minneapolis: Fortress Press, 1999), 21.

26. Ibid., 81.

27. Ibid., 89.

28. Carol Lee Sanchez, "Animal, Vegetable, and Mineral" in Adams, *Ecofeminism and the Sacred*, 223.

29. Victoria Tauli-Corpuz, "Reclaiming Earth-based Spirituality: Indigenous Women in the Cordillers," in Ruether, *Women Healing Earth*, 100–1.

30. Denise Ackerman and Tahira Joyner, "Earth-Healing in South Africa," in Ruether, *Women Healing Earth*, 126.

31. Teresa Berger, *Women's Ways of Worship: Gender Analysis and Liturgical History* (Collegeville, MN: Liturgical Press, 1999), 139–40.

32. Kwok Pui-lan, "Mending of Creation: Women, Nature, and Eschatological Hope," in Margaret A. Farley and Serene Jones, eds., *Liberating Eschatology, Essays in Honor of Letty M. Russell* (Louisville: Westminster John Knox Press, 1999), 148.

33. Marjorie Proctor-Smith, *Praying with Our Eyes Open: Engendering Feminist Liturgical Prayer* (Nashville: Abingdon, 1995), 143.

34. Andy Smith, "For All Those Who Were Indian in a Former Life," in Adams, *Ecofeminism and the Sacred*, 169.

35. Veronica Brady, "Preface," in Norman C. Habel, ed., *Readings from the Perspective of Earth: The Earth Bible Series, Volume One* (Cleveland, OH: Pilgrim Press, 2000), 13.

36. Patricia Milne, "No Promised Land: Rejecting the Authority of the Bible," in P. Trible, T. Frymer-Kensky, and P. J. Milne, eds., *Feminist Approaches to the Bible* (Washington: Biblical Archaeological Society, 1995), 70.

37. Patricia Milne, "The Patriarchal Stamp of Scripture: The Implications of Structural Analyses for Feminist Hermeneutics," in Athalya Brenner, ed., *A Feminist Companion to Genesis* (Sheffield, England: Sheffield Academic Press, 1993), 167.

38. Heather Eaton, "Ecofeminist Contributions to an Ecojustice Hermeneutics," in Habel, *Readings from the Perspective of Earth*, 59.

39. Anne Primavesi, *From Apocalypse to Genesis: Ecology, Feminism and Christianity* (Minneapolis: Fortress Press, 1991), 343–44.

40. Ibid., 334.

41. Excerpts of "The Woman I Love is a Planet; the Planet I Love is a Tree," by Paula Gunn Allen, from *Reweaving the World: The Emergence of Ecofeminism*, edited by Irene Diamond and Gloria Fenman Orenstein. Copyright © 1990 by Irene Diamond and Gloria Fenman Orenstein. Reprinted by permission of Sierra Club Books. She closes this section quoting the book of Proverbs.

42. Alice Walker, *In Search of Our Mothers' Gardens: Womanist Prose* (New York: Harcourt Brace Jovanovich, 1983), xii.

43. Alice Walker, "The Gospel According to Shug," in *Temple of My Familiar* (New York: Simon and Schuster, 1989), 288–89.

44. Marjorie Procter-Smith speaks of memory and imagination in *In Her Own Rite: Constructing Feminist Liturgical Tradition* (Nashville: Abingdon Press, 1990), 36–59.

45. Gabriele Uhlein, ed., *Meditations with Hildegard of Bingen* (Santa Fe, NM: Bear & Co., 1982), 45–46, 58, 78.

46. Carolyn McDade, "The Song of Community," *Rain Upon Dry Land* © 1984, Surtsey Publishing. Audio recording.

47. Rachel Carson, *The Sense of Wonder* (San Francisco: HarperCollins, 1956), 89.

two

THE ART OF CREATING ECOFEMINIST LITURGIES

The art of creating ecofeminist liturgies can be learned. Some people have a natural talent for creating liturgies, others have traditional training, and some have both. Feminist liturgy making and writing has developed guidelines gleaned from the experiences of feminist liturgical communities, from the trial and error of its practitioners, from traditional liturgical theory, and from cross-cultural ritual tradition.

Margaret Mead, well-known anthropologist, offers clues about how to create good ecofeminist liturgies:

> A good ritual . . . like a natural language . . . has been spoken for a very long time by very many kinds of people. . . .
> It must be old, otherwise it is not polished. It must be old, otherwise it cannot reflect the play of many imaginations.

It must be old, otherwise it will not be fully available to everyone born within that tradition. Yet it also must be alive and fresh, open to new vision and changed vision.

The essence of ritual is the ability of the known form to re-invoke past emotion. . . .

Celebrations answer the needs of each age: of the youngest child, first enthralled by the lights of candles on a cake; . . . of great-grandparents, living longer than people have ever lived and trying hard to learn how to remain in touch with the modern world. A celebration must be a ceremony in which each finds something of her/his own and all share something together. It must be a community ceremonial if it is to have a place for each of them. . . . If we are to have real celebrations that do not pall or peter out because of the shallowness of their inspiration, we must have an informed and exciting mix of the ceremonial inventions of other ages and other people. Only thus can the new sparkle like a jewel in a setting, which, because it is familiar, sets it off.[1]

I offer two processes for developing the art of creating ecofeminist liturgies. The first is a simple process for first-time planners to create a fifteen-to-twenty minute liturgy. The second is a more detailed process for seasoned planners. Both are offered as structures to make liturgy making easier and more accessible. Remember, designing liturgy is a creative process; so trust the creativity within yourself and within your community. Call forth the gifts of community members to enliven the liturgy—for example, musicians, dancers, artists, storytellers.

From my thirty years of liturgy planning I have learned that to create liturgies you only need time, thought, and resources. These guidelines may make your planning process more fruitful and/or give you courage to begin.

Listen to the needs of individuals and the community. Search with them and discuss a possible plan for the liturgy. Allow yourself a two- or three-hour block of time for an initial brainstorming to identify and select together meaningful symbols, texts, poems, music, gestures. Brainstorm together the content of the liturgy and design a first draft. Collect further ideas for the liturgical experience, consult with the individual/planners, follow up with one or two hours to refine and simplify your original ideas. Prepare the final liturgical text, noting who will lead which parts. Schedule about an hour to prepare materials, symbols, and the environment. Celebrate the liturgy. Evaluate what worked (what you would repeat again) and what did not work (what you would not do again). Edit the liturgical text to reflect how the liturgy happened. Tell the story; share the experience with other communities.

FIRST-TIME PLANNERS

Invite your creative, artistic, practical self to come to the fore. If you and your community are new to designing and celebrating liturgies, begin with one that is short and simple—about fifteen to twenty minutes long.

Choose a theme. Pick a reading and song that amplify this message. Gather in a circle. Place a small altar table (or cloth on the floor) in the center of the circle and rest a candle on it. Light the candle. Read the poem, story, or scripture passage. Share what it means and how you will put its message into action. Sing the song. Extinguish the candle.

You can vary this liturgical model by choosing a special symbol (object) that carries the message of your theme, resting it on your altar table and talking about it. Among the symbols you may want to use are water, fire, earth, oil, and harvest symbols. The following guides suggest ways participants can interact with such symbols.

Water: Pour water from a pitcher into a bowl in silence or while sharing a reflection on a theme like that from the World Water Day liturgy: "Call to mind the places on this Earth where the waters are polluted, troubled, or in drought. (*Pause*) Let us name them and pray, 'May all waters be healed.'"

Fire: Light a fire and invite each participant to add a stick in silence or express feelings on a question such as "What passion for ecojustice is burning inside me?"

Earth: Invite participants to pull a weed, put it into a compost pile, plant a seedling, and reflect on, "How am I caring for planet Earth?" See the liturgy "This Earth Is Sacred" for more details.

Oil: Invite participants to bless one another with the oil by massaging hands and sharing "What ecofeminist healing powers do I reclaim?"

Harvest symbols: Put corn, eggplant, apples, seeds, nuts, squash, gourds, and other harvest symbols in the center of the circle and invite participants to choose a symbol and reflect on it using a question like that from the liturgy "A Garden of Abundance": "What abundance do you have in your life and how are you returning blessing to all creation from what you have received?"

MORE PRACTICED PLANNERS

Think of the ecofeminist liturgy that your community needs.

Search with individuals or community members and discuss a possible plan. Be attentive to community events, global issues, seasonal changes, personal or individual reflections. Write down the major theme of the liturgy and give it a tentative name if you can. Once you have the initial idea, you will want to ascertain what other liturgies of the same theme already exist. They could be models for you. Check your resources, begin with those listed in the bibliography in this book, or contact WATER, the Women's Alliance for Theology, Ethics and Ritual.

Focus the theme.

Think of what you want this liturgy to say, why you are creating it, and what you want to happen to people during and after it. Jot down your initial words, phrases, and ideas. You are brainstorming, so let the energy flow. You will be able to reject, use, alter, or combine your ideas later. You are creating the raw material for the liturgy.

Discover a symbol that will visibly carry the message of the liturgy.

Symbols are key to successful liturgies. Reclaim symbols used by many traditions, such as oil, bread, water, candles, and ashes. Try others, such as a variety of breads and drinks, harvest symbols, sticks, feathers, ribbons, rocks, and shells. Choose one symbol. Keep it simple.

Identify readings, prayers, and blessings that make your message concrete.

What do you want them to say? Whose words do you want to hear—scripture, poetry, excerpts by women from international and cross-cultural settings? Should these be mimed, danced, read chorally, spoken with many voices? Do you need to write new prayers, blessings, or stories? Be sure that they are in or changed to inclusive language.

Select music that conveys your message.

Identify songs, chants, and instrumental and taped music that support your theme. Note the mood and message to decide the appropriate place for each in your service. Use women's music whenever possible to educate others about it.

Choose an environment that enhances the theme of the celebration.

This could be outside near water, in a park or garden, in a special room, at someone's house, or in a church or chapel. Arrange the seating in a circle around a circular table. Be attentive to color and its coordination with candles, cloths, symbols, and banners. Place the liturgical objects on the table or decide to bring them into the liturgy at an appropriate time.

Share the leadership for various parts of the service with several people.
The liturgy belongs to the community; therefore, it is not centered in one person. There is no main presider, rather various parts need to be initiated by different people. Decide who will lead each section. Give the leaders scripts and ideas to guide them in their parts, but encourage them to use their own words for introductions, blessings, and prayers.

Include body expression.
Use postures and gestures to embody the message of the liturgy, such as movement to music, dance/choreography that includes hand motions or bowing, and warm embraces at the time of peace sharing. Use dramatic gestures when interacting with the symbols, for example, pour the water like a waterfall. In the course of the liturgy you may light a candle, wash your hands, break bread, drink from a cup, share herbs, plant bulbs, meditate on the colors of summer, or pray with your arms crossed in front of your chest swaying side to side.

Involve children in the celebration.
Invite children to be with the community at the beginning of the liturgy. Then after the readings gather them in another space to create the same symbol that focuses the liturgy. For a harvest liturgy help them draw harvest symbols or carve pumpkins; for a spring liturgy help them plant seeds. Have them return to the liturgy at a later time to share their symbols.

Be attentive to moments of transition in the liturgy.
Check the transition moments in the liturgy. When one part flows smoothly into the next the liturgy works. This is done best by sounds appealing to the senses, not by announcement.

DESIGNING THE ECOFEMINIST LITURGICAL STRUCTURE

When the previous brainstorming is complete, it is time to create the order of the liturgy. The best liturgies, prayers, and blessings come from the heart and are centered in feminist sources and feminist liturgical theory. They draw the community in as witnesses and as participants. I have discovered the following to be an effective structure for a liturgy.

Preparation

Create the space and ambience to reflect the message of the liturgy. An example from "Welcome Spring Renewal":

> Place together on a table a pot with soil, a pitcher of water, and seven herb clippings or seedlings. (Invite participants to bring herbs from their gardens.) Plan the ceremony to be outside in order to unite fully with the rebirthing energy of the Earth.

Call to Gather

Welcome participants. Focus the liturgy, state why you are celebrating this theme, and invite people to gather. An example from "Welcome Spring Renewal":

> Welcome to our celebration of the fullness of spring. This is the season of reawakening to quickening life, the time when green beauty returns to the Earth. New leaves bud on tree branches, the birds return in song, the animal and plant species give birth to their next generations, and colorful flowers burst forth anew each day. Spring is the season of rebirth and the promise of new beginnings. Today we gather to "Welcome Spring Renewal" and give thanks for the beauty and renewal of this time.

Naming the Circle

Invite participants to share their names, where they are from and/ or something that focuses the liturgy. For example, for the "Welcome

Spring Renewal" liturgy participants are invited to "speak your name and share what activity you like to do to celebrate the return of spring."

Music / Song / Chant

Be attentive to what mood you want to establish—quiet, festive, haunting, soothing. Music, songs, and chants can be used in a variety of places in the liturgy. In "Welcome Spring Renewal" the song "The Flower Carol" was sung after the prayer and before the first reading.

Prayer / Litany

Write or choose a prayer or litany that could form a transition into the reading, be a general address to the Spirit for openness, or focus the theme of the liturgy. In "Welcome Spring Renewal" I used "We Give-Away Our Thanks," which Dolores La Chapelle wrote.

Readings

Choose one or two readings that will be central to the liturgy. These can be scripture passages, poems, excerpts from writings on ecology and ecofeminism, or stories. If your group is scripture focused, you will want to choose a scriptural text from a feminist perspective. A sung or spoken refrain can be used to connect the readings and deepen the message. In "Welcome Spring Renewal" I chose three poems and used the chant "The Earth, the Air, the Fire, the Water / Return, return, return, return" after each to amplify and embody the theme.

Reflection

This is traditionally the homily, sermon, or preaching time. Since Creator Spirit speaks to everyone, the sharing is communal. Offer a few sentences that recap the message of the readings. Then pose one or two questions for reflection. Depending on the size of the group, form small groups or share in the whole gathering. The reflection from "Welcome Spring Renewal" follows:

"'Once in spring, I with God had a quiet talk.' During spring-time the Holy One seems very near. How do you experience God, Creator Spirit, Wisdom Sophia in spring? What do you talk about with the Holy One? What healing is needed this spring within you, on planet Earth? (*Sharing*)"

Song Refrain

If people are meeting in groups they need more than the spoken human voice to gather them back as a whole. Singing a song refrain that has already been a part of the service invites attention and brings closure to this section. In "Welcome Spring Renewal," the chant "The Earth, the Air, the Fire, the Water" called people back to the whole community.

Presentation of the Symbol

Name the symbol, touch it, show it to the group, and say why you are using it. In "Welcome Spring Renewal" the symbol was herbs. The leader presented the herbs, saying, "Creation shares power and beauty by giving us healing herbs. (*The leader takes some herbs.*) Touch these herbs with me."

Blessing the Symbol

Bless the symbol. For the blessing in "Welcome Spring Renewal" the leader prayed:

Blessed are you, Source of All Life and Beauty,
For giving us these herbs.
Air, fire, water, and spirit combine to bring them to life.
Bless us with the power of creation
That we may bless and be blessed by life.

(*The leader passes the herbs around for all to take some.*)

Interaction with Symbol

Give directions about how to interact with the symbol. Specify how to pass the symbol: around the circle, one person offers it to others, stations/centers, several people start passing to different parts of the circle, groups of people come forward to drink water from the common well. Be specific so that people will feel comfortable. In "Welcome Spring Renewal" participants were invited to plant the herb seeds: "This is the season of renewal and promise of new life, the time of rebirth and new beginnings. What do I wish for this spring? Let us plant the herbs and share a springtime wish. (*Planting and sharing*)"

Song
Use a song during or after the sharing of the symbol. In "Welcome Spring Renewal" the chant "The Earth, the Air, the Fire, the Water" was sung after the planting of the herbs.

Sending Forth
Pay careful attention to the closure. When the liturgy ends abruptly, people can be left with an unresolved feeling. The Sending Forth gathers up the message of the liturgy and challenges people to go forth to act on it. I usually offer this challenging closure in three sentences or three parts. To close "Welcome Spring Renewal," I wrote:

Let us join with the Earth and with each other

> To bring new life to the land
> To restore the waters
> To refresh the air

> To protect the animals
> To treasure the trees
> To gaze at the stars

> To cherish the human community
> To heal the Earth
> To remember the children

Let us go forth to put our words into action.

Greeting of Peace

I usually like the Greeting of Peace at the end of the liturgy to bring closure. People have created something together and want to bid farewell with hugs, handshakes, warm greetings.

Song

Use a closing song that invites a spiral or circle dance so people can embrace, sway, and dance.

CONCLUSION

I began with memory and imagination. I end with transformation. These clues at how to do ecofeminist liturgies are an invitation to readers and communities to use the many resources available to us to heal women and the Earth.

Take ecofeminist liturgies to the city streets and
   country roads of the world!
Let us go forth in all directions of the universe to bless
   and to embrace, to resist, and to heal.
Let us go forth in the name of Wisdom Sophia,
   Creator Spirit, to transform the world!
Amen. Blessed be. Let it be so.

NOTES

1. Margaret Mead, "Celebration: A Human Need," *The Catechist* (May 1976), 54.

partone

SPRING *returning to life*

I, the fiery life of divine wisdom,
I ignite the beauty of the plains,
I sparkle in the waters,
and I burn in the sun, and the moon, and the stars . . .
with wisdom I order all rightly.

— Hildegard of Bingen,
Meditations with Hildegard of Bingen

In God's hand is the life of every living thing, and the
breath of every human being.

— Job 12:10

To think Green is nothing less than to heal
the human spirit and completely reallocate our
resources and priorities. We need nothing less
if we are to survive and flourish in the
twenty-first century.

— Petra Kelly,
Thinking Green!

Spring returns, again. The Spirits of Renewal and Rebirth wake up. In the beginning is the awakening . . . the changing light . . . returning birds . . . warm breezes . . . budding trees . . . breathing, stretching, pushing, grunting, and struggling to come to life.

Along with the natural world our spirits awaken from a long winter sleep. It is time for new life and renewal to emerge within and around us. The returning green power opens our senses to the life-death-rebirth cycle of this season of hope. We see daffodils blooming and lightning flashing across the sky, hear birds chirping and thunder crashing, smell sweet fragrances and rainstorms, touch tulips and flood waters, and taste fresh herbs and broken bread. Spring is the season to notice the beauty and power of the Earth and to work to ensure that they continue. The buds and blossoms of the season can inspire wonder. The new rain and fresh green, growing plants can invoke celebration.

The ecofeminist liturgies in this section focus on the themes of new beginnings, rebirth, renewal, inspiration, reawakening, and germination. They use the symbols of bulbs, seeds, seedlings, herbs, eggs, kites, spring wreaths, and Easter baskets. They urge us to heal the Earth in spring by working in the garden, using compost to fertilize soil, hanging a birdfeeder, planting trees and groundcover, making a pond with a fountain, cultivating flowers, herbs, and vegetables, cleaning up waterways, or taking a walk to enjoy the beauty of the Earth. Use them as models to celebrate the spring festivals: March 21 (September 21), vernal or spring equinox; March 22, World Water Day; April 22, Earth Day; April 26, Arbor Day; May 1 (October 31), May Day, Beltane, Mary's month.

three

WELCOME SPRING RENEWAL

Spring arrives each year about March 21 or September 21, depending on your location. This vernal equinox is one of the four seasonal shifts based on the sun's elliptic relationship to the celestial equator of the Earth. On this day both night and day are in complete balance. Light and dark are equal: twelve hours each. Spring officially begins. This is the day the ancient Chinese balanced eggs on end to welcome spring. During this season, Easter, using the fertility symbols of colorful eggs and hopping bunnies, celebrates the resurrection of the Christ. Spring festivals celebrate rebirth and renewal.

This liturgy welcomes spring, the time of renewal and promise of new life, of rebirth and new beginnings. It invites reflection on how we experience God, Creator Spirit, Wisdom Sophia, in spring. It calls forth sharing and action about personal and global qualities that need to be brought into harmony.

Preparation

Place together on a table a pot with soil, a pitcher of water, and seven herb clippings or seedlings. (Invite participants to bring herbs from their gardens.) Plan the ceremony to be outside in order to unite fully with the rebirthing energy of the Earth.

Call to Gather

Welcome to our celebration of the fullness of spring. This is the season of reawakening to quickening life, the time when green beauty returns to the Earth. New leaves bud on tree branches, the birds return in song, the animal and plant species give birth to their next generations, and colorful flowers burst forth anew each day. Spring is the season of rebirth and the promise of new beginnings. Today we gather to "Welcome Spring Renewal" and give thanks for the beauty and renewal of this time.

Naming the Circle

To create our circle, speak your name and share what activity you like to do to celebrate the return of spring. *(Sharing)*

Prayer: "We Give-Away Our Thanks," by Dolores La Chapelle

Let us pray:
> We give-away our thanks to the earth
> which gives us our home.
> We give-away our thanks to the rivers and lakes
> which give-away their water.
> We give-away our thanks to the trees
> which give-away fruit and nuts.
> We give-away our thanks to the wind
> which brings rain to water the plants.
> We give-away our thanks to the sun
> who gives-away warmth and light.

All beings on earth: the trees, the animals, the wind,
    and the rivers
  give-away to one another so all is in balance.
We give-away our promise to begin to learn
  how to stay in balance with all the earth.[1]

Touch the Earth
Choose one of the seven herbs, take it into your hands, listen to it
and honor it. Herbs have been used by generations of Earthlings
for food, medicine, and good luck. Herbs heal, cast spells, and
nourish body and soul.

Song: "The Flower Carol," traditional, tune "Good King Wenceslas"
  Spring has now unwrapped the flowers, day is fast reviving.
  Life in all her growing powers toward the light is striving.
  Gone the iron touch of cold, winter time and frost time.
  Seedlings working through the mold
      now make up for lost time.

  Herb and plant that winter long slumbered at their leisure,
  Now bestirring green and strong, find in growth their pleasure.
  All the world with beauty fills, gold the green enhancing.
  Flowers make glee among the hills
      and set the meadows dancing.

  Through each wonder of fair days life herself expresses.
  Beauty follows all her ways as the world she blesses.
  So as she renews the earth, artist without rival,
  In her grace of glad new birth,
  We must seek revival.[2]

Thought of Spring: "Everywhere Is the Green of New Growth,"
Chinook Psalter
(Different participants read quotes. After each one, everyone chants.)
READER ONE: Everywhere is the green of new growth,
    the amazing sight of the renewal of the earth.

We watch the grass once again emerging from the ground.
We notice the bright green atop the dark green on the pine,
    the fir, the hemlock, the spruce, the cedar.
The alder is already in leaf.
The old plum trees still blossom, leaf, and give forth fruit.
The locust is late as always.
Everywhere and always the song of birds . . . bees raiding the
orchard, raccoon prowling at nightfall, the earthworm
tunneling the garden, chickens and rabbits pecking and
nibbling, the goats tugging to reach new delights . . . all are
the ubiquitous energies of life.

O God,
May we today be touched by grace, fascinated and moved by
       this your creation, energized by the power of
       new growth at work in your world.
May we move beyond viewing this life only through
      a frame, but
      touch it and be touched by it,
      know it and be known by it,
      love it and be loved by it.
May our bodies, our minds, our spirits, learn a new rhythm
      paced by the rhythmic pulse of the whole created order.
May spring come to us, be in us, and recreate life in us.[3]

Chant: "The Earth, the Air, the Fire, the Water," source unknown
The Earth, the Air, the Fire, the Water,
Return, return, return, return.[4]

Thought of Spring: "Over Cherry Blossoms ..." by Shuntaro Tanikawa
READER TWO: Over cherry blossoms
    white clouds
    over clouds
    the deep sky

over cherry blossoms
over clouds
over the sky
I can climb on forever

once in spring
I with god
had a quiet talk.[5]

Chant

The Earth, the Air, the Fire, the Water,
Return, return, return, return.

Thought of Spring: "Flowers Have Come," by Nezahualcoyotl

READER THREE: Flowers have come!
to refresh
and delight you, princes and princesses.

You see them briefly
as they dress themselves,
spread their petals,
perfect only in spring—
countless golden flowers!

The flowers have come
to the skirt of the mountain!

Yellow flowers
sweet flowers precious vanilla flowers the crows dark
    magic flowers
weave themselves together.

They are your
flowers, god.
We only borrow them:
your flowered drum,

your bells,
your song.
They are your
flowers, god.[6]

Chant

The Earth, the Air, the Fire, the Water,
Return, return, return, return.

Reflection

"Once in spring, I with God had a quiet talk." During springtime the Holy One seems very near. How do you experience God, Creator Spirit, Wisdom Sophia in spring? What do you talk about with the Holy One? What healing is needed this spring within you, on planet Earth? *(Sharing)*

Blessing the Herbs

Creation shares power and beauty by giving us healing herbs. *(The leader takes some herbs.)* Touch these herbs with me.

Blessed are you, Source of All Life and Beauty,
For giving us these herbs.
Air, fire, water, and spirit combine to bring them to life.
Bless us with the power of creation
That we may bless and be blessed by life.

(The leader passes the herbs around for all to take some.)

Planting the Herbs

This is the season of renewal and promise of new life, the time of rebirth and new beginnings. What do I wish for this spring? Let us plant the herbs and share a springtime wish. *(Planting and sharing)*

Chant

The Earth, the Air, the Fire, the Water,
Return, return, return, return.

Sending Forth

Let us join with the Earth and with each other
To bring new life to the land
To restore the waters
To refresh the air

To protect the animals
To treasure the trees
To gaze at the stars

To cherish the human community
To heal the Earth
To remember the children
Let us go forth to put our words into action.

Song: "The Seven Herbs of Spring," words by Rowan Wild Vine, music traditional Scottish

I must go and pick me the seven herbs of spring,
Nor wait for my washing, nor any other thing,
But gather them together for the healing that they bring.
A summons from the Mother are the seven herbs of spring.

Oh, oh, oh the Lady oh! She walks with Her basket
swinging to and fro.
The seed sift through and her clogs break up the grass,
And her holy weeds flourish where e'er the Lady pass.[7]

NOTES

1. In Dolores La Chapelle, *Earth Festivals: Seasonal Celebrations for Everyone Young and Old* (Silverton, CO: Finn Hill Arts, 1974), 212.

2. The words are based on a translation of the original Latin.

3. "Everywhere Is the Green of New Growth," *Chinook Psalter,* in Roberts and Amidon, *Earth Prayers,* 292–93.

4. "The Earth, the Air, the Fire, the Water," source unknown, Libana, *A Circle Is Cast* © 1986, Libana, Inc., P.O. Box 400530, Cambridge, MA 02140. 800-997-7757. www.libana.com. Audio recording.

5. Shuntaro Tanikawa, "Over Cherry Blossoms . . ." in *The Selected Poems of Shuntaro Tanikawa,* trans. Harold Wright (Northpoint Press, 1983). Permission granted through the office of Bonnie R. Crown, International Literature and Arts. Also appears in Roberts and Amidon, *Earth Prayers,* 295.

6. Nezahualcoyotl, "Flowers Have Come," in Roberts and Amidon, *Earth Prayers,* 302.

7. Rowan Wild Vine (words), "The Seven Herbs of Spring" (music traditional Scottish), reprinted from *Songs for Earthlings,* ed. Julie Forest Middleton (Philadelphia: Emerald Earth Publishing, 1998), 170.

four

WATER TO MAKE ALL THINGS NEW

March 22, World Water Day, calls attention to a precious resource. All nations require a safe, plentiful supply. Water, from which all life emerges, has innate properties to sustain that life, quench thirst, cleanse, purify, and restore clarity.

This liturgy invites participants to connect with water, listen to the sounds of water, pray for a healing of the waters, and bless their bodies with water. It is a restorative ceremony.

Preparation

Gather in a circle outside near water, if possible: a lake, the ocean, a river, a waterfall, a swimming pool, or a fountain. Place in the center a bowl or a child's wading pool with a little water in it, a pitcher of water, and a rain stick.

Call to Gather

(One plays a musical instrument such as a rain stick and speaks:)

Come to the water. *(Leader gestures for all to gather in a circle around or near the water.)* There is a time for everything and today, March 22, World Water Day, we give thanks for the precious resource of water, the life-giving element of nature from which all life emerges. Water refreshes, soothes, and anoints the parched body and dry Earth.

This bowl (pool) of water *(leader stands and touches it or holds it, showing it to the gathered)* signifies the well or spring, the traditional meeting place of women and the home of spirits, goddesses, and healing energies. Sources of water are sacred.

Today we call attention to the global water crisis. As we pour water *(leader picks up a pitcher and pours water into the basin)*, we know from the United Nations that during the 1990s 1.23 billion people did not have adequate access to clean drinking water; 2.1 billion people did not have access to adequate sanitation. Those numbers are increasing, and women suffer because women worldwide are the family caretakers. Many women in the Two-Thirds World carry heavy loads of water long distances, three to six hours per day, from remote water sources. They spend hours purifying it. And when children or family members become sick from waterborne diseases, women spend another portion of their lives caring for the ill and dying. All creation needs clean, safe water.

Today we gather to give thanks for water and pray for "Water to Make All Things New."

Naming the Circle

Let us form our circle by speaking our names, passing the bowl of water (or touching the pool), and sharing how we are connected to water in our lives. If you need healing, dip your fingers in the water and sprinkle your face, wrists, or head with a few drops. (*Naming and sharing*)

Listening to Water

Water, life giving, life threatening, life blessing. Listen to sounds of water. (*All listen to the natural water sounds: one plays the rain stick; another pours water from a pitcher into the water bowl or pool.*)

Song: "Living Water," by Colleen Fulmer

> Come, you hungry, come, you thirsty;
> Drink living water, come to the well.
> Come, you weary, bring your burdens;
> Drink living water, come to the well.
>
> Vengan, hambrientos, vengan sedientos;
> Tomen agua viva, vengan a mi.
> Vengan, cansados, vengan agobiados;
> Tomen agua viva, vengan a mi.
>
> Come, you wounded, bring your suffering;
> Drink living water, come to the well.
> Vengan, los pobres, vengan los humildes;
> Tomen agua viva, vengan a mi.[1]

(*Add verses that reflect the mood of the group.*)

Healing the Waters

Some waters need healing. Call to mind the places on this Earth where the waters are polluted, troubled, or in drought. (*Pause*) Let us name them and pray, "May all waters be healed."

LEADER: In the Two-Thirds World hauling water is one of women's main daily occupations.

RESPONSE: **May all waters be healed.**

LEADER: Many people in large cities worldwide do not drink water out of the faucets because the water is polluted.

RESPONSE: **May all waters be healed.**

LEADER: In Bangladesh there is a new disaster: wells pump poison and people die from arsenic.

RESPONSE: **May all waters be healed.**

LEADER: The Bagmati River in Kathmandu is characteristically dirty brown and full of particles that carry waterborne diseases.

RESPONSE: **May all waters be healed.**

LEADER: Many urban areas in the United States are working to clean up their rivers: Atlanta's Chatahoochee, Cincinnati's Mill Creek, Denver's South Platte, Washington, D.C.'s Anacostia.

RESPONSE: **May all waters be healed.**

LEADER: In many parts of rural India women walk many miles in search of water because the rivers are dammed to irrigate commodity crops like sugarcane.

RESPONSE: **May all waters be healed.**

LEADER: Crossing the Andes, bus drivers routinely throw styrofoam trash into the rivers.

RESPONSE: **May all waters be healed.**

LEADER: In many parts of Africa the rains fail and drought prevails.

RESPONSE: **May all waters be healed.**

LEADER: Name other problems now and we will respond. (*Naming*)

Prayer

Let us pray:
> Spirit of Renewal, breathe into all waters.
> Waters, be made clean that you may fully praise our Creator
> And share your life-giving powers with all creation.
> Source of Life, Living Water, Restoring Creator Spirit,
> heal all waters.
> Amen. Blessed be. Let it be so.

Reading: "He Na Tye Woman," by Paula Gunn Allen

> Water.
> Lakes and rivers.
> Oceans and streams.
> Springs, pools and gullies.
> Arroyos, creeks, watersheds.
> Pacific. Atlantic. Mediterranean.
> Indian. Caribbean. China Sea.
> (Lying. Dreaming on shallow shores.)
> Arctic. Antarctic. Baltic.
> Mississippi. Amazon. Columbia. Nile.
> Thames. Sacramento. Snake. (Undulant woman river.)
> Seine. Rio Grande. Willamette. McKenzie. Ohio.
> Hudson. Po. Rhine. Rhone.
> Rain. After a lifetime of drought.
> That finally cleanses the air.
> The soot from our eyes.
> The dingy windows of our western home.
> The rooftops and branches. The wings of birds.
> The new light on a slant. Pouring. Making everything new.[2]

Chant: "The River Is Flowing," by Diana Hildebrand-Hull

> The river is flowing, flowing and growing,
> The river she is flowing, down to the sea.

Mother, carry me, your child I will always be,
Mother, carry me, down to the sea.[3]

Litany of Water

Wisdom Sophia, the Source of Life, connects with water to bless creation. Let us remember the presence of Creator Spirit through water and respond: "Blessed are you, Source of Life."

LEADER: Your spirit moves over the waters at creation.

RESPONSE: **Blessed are you, Source of Life.**

LEADER: You form new life in the waters of the womb.

RESPONSE: **Blessed are you, Source of Life.**

LEADER: You renew the Earth with winter snows and spring rains.

RESPONSE: **Blessed are you, Source of Life.**

LEADER: You share life-giving water with your creation.

RESPONSE: **Blessed are you, Source of Life.**

LEADER: You dance your people through water to promised lands.

RESPONSE: **Blessed are you, Source of Life.**

LEADER: You weep with us over the violence creation experiences from abusers.

RESPONSE: **Blessed are you, Source of Life.**

LEADER: You water our gardens to bring forth food.

RESPONSE: **Blessed are you, Source of Life.**

LEADER: What else do we want to bless? Tell us and we will respond. (*Sharing*)

RESPONSE: **Blessed are you, Source of Life.**

Blessing the Water

(*One gestures for all participants to come to the well, then speaks.*) Let us each pour water from a pitcher into the bowl (pool). (*Pouring*) Let us bless this water together. Extend your hands and pray each line after me.

> Blessed are you, Source of Life, Wisdom Sophia, Creator of the Universe, (*Echo*)
> For you give all creation water to make all things new. (*Echo*)
> Cleanse all waters. Multiply our water sources. Bless the Earth with water. (*Echo*)
> Bless us with life-giving water. Refresh the thirsty with safe water. Restore all waters. (*Echo*)
> Amen. Blessed be. Let it be so. (*Echo*)

Blessing Ourselves

Let us bless ourselves with water. Touch the water. (*Pause*) Think of a part of the body you would like to bless. (*Pause*) Let us bless our bodies. (*The leader begins and ends the blessing.*)

Touch your mouth and say after me: "Bless my mouth that I may speak truthfully." (*Echo. Repeat this pattern for other body parts. For example, "Bless my ears that I may hear the sounds of water."*)

Let us face outward with our hands extended to the world, saying: "Bless the Earth with water." (*Echo*)

Let us bless one another, using a water gesture like falling rain. (*Blessing*)

Song: "Come, Drink Deep," by Carolyn McDade

> Come drink deep of living waters
> Without cup bend close to the ground
> Wade with bare feet into troubled waters
> Where love of life abounds.
>
> I turn my head to sky rains falling
> Wash the wounds of numbness from my soul,
> Turn my heart in tides of fierce renewal
> Where love and rage run whole.

Come rains of heaven on the dry seed
Rains of love on every tortured land
Roots complacent awaken in compassion
So hope springs in our hands
Come drink deep.[4]

Sending Forth

May Wisdom Sophia, the Source of Life,
Heal and renew all water supplies.
May Wisdom Sophia, the Source of Healing,
Send gentle rains upon dry lands.
May Wisdom Sophia, the Source of Eternal Rest,
Return all life peacefully to the sea.

Let us open our circle.

NOTES

1. Colleen Fulmer, "Living Water," *Her Wings Unfurled* © 1989, Heartbeats. Audio recording.

2. Paula Gunn Allen, "He Na Tye Woman," in *Shadow Country* (Oakland, CA: Regents of University of California, 1982), 123–25.

3. Diana Hildebrand-Hull, "The River is Flowing," reprinted from Middleton, *Songs for Earthlings*, 34.

4. Carolyn McDade, "Come, Drink Deep," *Rain Upon Dry Land* ©1984, Surtsey Publishing. Audio recording.

five

THINK GREEN AS HOPE FOR PLANET EARTH

Earth Day, April 22, is set aside to remind us to cherish planet Earth. In order for earth, air, fire, and water to stay in balance, Earthlings need to pay attention to ecofriendly living and act in Earth-centered ways. All over the world people are making connections between ecology and their own lives.

This liturgy invites participants to experience an interconnection with the pain and power of creation. It challenges all to think green and live an ecologically sensitive lifestyle to help the planet survive.

Preparation

Celebrate this liturgy outside, or in a room with many windows. Spread an earth-colored cloth in the center of the circle; on and around it place symbols from Earth, such as a bowl of soil, rocks, flowers, leaves, a bowl of water, a loaf of bread, glasses of juice and wine, a basket of nuts and fruits, and a world globe. Duplicate, cut separately, and pass around the group the quotes that participants will read during the "Thoughts of Green" section.

Call to Gather

Welcome to our celebration of Earth Day. Earth is a sacred space of ever-greening life. Trees, springs, mountains,. flowers, animals, and humans live on her and call her home. Each teaches us about living and dying. All creation is interconnected. Planet Earth needs our respect and care. She is our sister/mother/friend/companion who stuns us with beauty and life-giving power.

Naming the Circle

Let us take time to create our community and unite ourselves with all creation. Take the globe, speak your name, say what you are thinking about this Earth Day, and pass the globe to the person on your left. (*When the globe returns to the person who first passed it, that person places it in the center of the circle.*)

Prayer of Creation: "We Call upon the Earth, Our Planet Home," Chinook Blessing Litany

Let us pray, alternating sides:

SIDE ONE: We call upon the earth, our planet home,
　　with its beautiful depths and soaring heights,
　　its vitality and abundance of life,
　　and together we ask that it:

ALL: Teach us, and show us the way.

SIDE TWO: We call upon the mountains, the Cascades
and the Olympics,
the high green valleys and meadows filled with wild flowers,
the snows that never melt, the summits of intense silence,
and we ask that they:

ALL: Teach us, and show us the way.

SIDE ONE: We call upon the waters that rim the earth,
horizon to horizon,
that flow in our rivers and streams,
that fall upon our gardens and fields,
and we ask that they:

ALL: Teach us, and show us the way.

SIDE TWO: We call upon the land, which grows our food,
the nurturing soil, the fertile fields,
the abundant gardens and orchards,
and we ask that they:

ALL: Teach us, and show us the way.

SIDE ONE: We call upon the forests, the great trees
reaching strongly to the sky with earth in their roots
and the heavens in their branches,
the fir and the pine and the cedar,
and we ask them to:

ALL: Teach us, and show us the way.

SIDE TWO: We call upon the creatures of the fields and forests
and seas,
our brothers and sisters the wolves and deer,
the eagle and dove, the great whales and the dolphin,
the beautiful Orca and salmon who share our Northwest home,
and we ask them to:

ALL: Teach us, and show us the way.

SIDE ONE: We call upon all those who have lived on this earth,
   our ancestors and our friends,
   who dreamed the best for future generations,
   and upon whose lives our lives are built,
   and with thanksgiving, we call upon them to:

ALL: Teach us, and show us the way.

SIDE TWO: And lastly, we call upon all that we hold most sacred,
   the presence and power of the Great Spirit of love and truth
   which flows through all the universe . . .
   to be with us to:

ALL: Teach us, and show us the way.[1]

Touch the Earth

Choose a symbol of Earth from the center of the circle, take it in
your hands carefully, listen to it, and honor it. Let us collectively
dance around the circle using a stepping pattern of right footstep
right, left footstep close, while singing:

> We are a wheel,
> a circle of life.
> We are a wheel,
> a circle of power.

> We are a wheel,
> a circle of light.
> Circling the world,
> this sacred hour.[2]

Thoughts of Green

*Different participants read the quotes. After each three everyone chants
"The Earth, the Air, the Fire, the Water"(source unknown).*

READER: I shall remind you of the works of God, and tell you
what I have seen. . . . Who could ever grow tired of gazing on
God's glory? (Sirach 42:15, 25)

READER: To think green is nothing less than to heal the human spirit and completely reallocate our resources and priorities. We need nothing less if we are to survive and flourish in the twenty-first century. (Petra Kelly, *Thinking Green!*)[3]

READER: The decaying state of nature as well as the growing gap between the rich and the poor point to the need for an ecological theology of liberation, one that can free us from insatiable consumerism and, as a result, liberate others, including the natural world, for a better, healthier life. (Sallie McFague, *Life Abundant*)[4]

Chant

The Earth, the Air, the Fire, the Water,
Return, return, return, return.
The Earth, the Air, the Fire, the Water,
Return, return, return, return, return.[5]

READER: Is this not a precious home for us Earthlings? Is this not worth our love? Does it not deserve all the inventiveness and courage and generosity of which we are capable to preserve it from degradation and destruction and, by doing so, to secure our own survival? (Barbara Ward and Rene Dubos, *Only One Earth*)[6]

READER: Breaking the spirit of nature today through rape and violence done to the Earth, and breaking the spirit of nineteenth-century slave women through rape and violence, constitute crimes against nature and against the human spirit. . . . This defilement of nature's body and of black women's bodies is sin, since its occurrence denies that black women and nature are made in the image of God. Its occurrence is an assault upon the spirit of creation in women and nature. (Delores Williams, "Sin, Nature, and Black Women's Bodies")[7]

READER: This earth is my sister; I love her daily grace, her silent daring, and how loved I am, how we admire this strength in each other, all that we have lost, all that we have suffered, all that we know: we are stunned by this beauty, and I do not forget: what she is to me, what I am to her. (Susan Griffin, *Woman and Nature*)[8]

Chant

> The Earth, the Air, the Fire, the Water,
> Return, return, return, return.
> The Earth, the Air, the Fire, the Water,
> Return, return, return, return, return.

READER: There are people who think that only people have emotions like pride, fear, and joy, but those who know will tell you all things are alive, perhaps not in the same way we are alive, but each in its own way, as should be, for we are not all the same. And though different from us in shape and life span, different in Time and Knowing, yet are trees alive. And rocks. And water. And all know emotion. (Anne Cameron, *Daughters of Copper Woman*)[9]

READER: Glance at the sun.
> See the moon and the stars.
> Gaze at the beauty of earth's greeting.
> Now,
> think.
> What delight
> God gives
> to humankind
> with all these things. (Hildegard of Bingen, "Glance at the Sun")[10]

READER: Our thoughts must be on how to restore to the Earth its dignity as a living being; how to stop raping and plundering it as a matter of course. We must begin to develop the conscious-ness that everything has equal rights because existence itself is

equal. In other words, we are all here: trees, people, snakes, alike.
... [B]eyond feeding and clothing and sheltering ourselves, even
abundantly, we should be allowed to destroy only what we ourselves can re-create. We cannot re-create this world. We cannot
re-create "wilderness." We cannot even, truly, re-create ourselves.
Only our behavior can we re-create, or create anew. (Alice
Walker, "Everything is a Human Being")[11]

Chant

> The Earth, the Air, the Fire, the Water,
> Return, return, return, return.
> The Earth, the Air, the Fire, the Water,
> Return, return, return, return, return.

Reflection

How do you experience an interconnection with the pain and the
power of creation? Let us reflect silently for a few moments. (Pause)

Call to Partnership with All Relations:
"We Hear You, Fellow-Creatures," by Joanna Macy

We hear you, fellow-creatures. We know we are wrecking the
world and we are afraid. Don't leave us alone, we need your help.
You need us too, for your own survival. Are there powers you can
share with us?

"I, lichen, work slowly, very slowly. Time is my friend. This is
what I give you: patience for the long haul and perseverance."

"It is a dark time. As deep-diving trout I offer you my fear-
lessness of the dark."

"I, lion, give you my roar, the voice to speak out and be heard."

"I am caterpillar. The leaves I eat taste bitter now. But dimly I
sense a great change coming. What I offer you, humans, is my
willingness to dissolve and transform. I do that without knowing
what the end-result will be; so I share with you my courage too."[12]

Reflection

What green powers can you share to restore the Earth's dignity and help the planet survive? Let us share our reflections. *(Sharing)*

Blessing the Fruits of the Earth

Creation shares power by giving us daily food. *(The leader takes the basket of fruits, nuts, bread, juice, and wine.)* Extend your hands, palms up, and let us bless these fruits of the Earth together. Please pray after me.

> Blessed are you, Source of Nourishment, *(Echo)*
> For creating these fruits of the Earth *(Echo)*
> And sharing manna with your people as they wandered in
>   the desert. *(Echo)*
> Air, fire, water, earth, and spirit combined to make this food.
>   *(Echo)*
> Numberless beings have died and labored that we may eat.
>   *(Echo)*
> Nourish us with the power of creation that we may
>   nourish life. *(Echo)*

(The leader passes the basket around for all to take and eat.)

Dance of Blessing

Let us form an inner and an outer circle with partners facing each other and palms touching and mirroring. Let us close with a dance of blessing. *(Directions are for the inner circle; the outer circle follows using the opposite hand. The dance continues until the circle makes one rotation.)*

Chant: "O Great Spirit," traditional Native American

> O, Great Spirit, *(Left hand circles up, out, and to center)*
> Earth, Sun, Sky, and Sea: *(Right hand circles up, out, and to center)*
> You are inside *(Partners, palms touching, bow to each other)*
> And all around me. *(Partners let go of hands and turn left
>   to touch palms with a new partner.)*

O Great Spirit, Earth, Sun, Sky, and Sea
You are inside and all around me.[13]

Sending Forth

(The leader gestures for everyone to join hands and form a circle.)

I who am the source of all life, I send you forth
to manifest life for all the Earth.
Blessed be life. Please echo this after me.
Blessed be life. *(Echo)*

I who am the beauty of all life, I send you forth
to manifest beauty for all the Earth.
Blessed be beauty. *(Echo)*

I who am the power of all life, I send you forth
to manifest power for all the Earth.
Blessed be power. *(Echo)*

I who am the truth of all life, I send you forth
to manifest truth for all the Earth.
Blessed be truth. *(Echo)*

I who am the energy of all life, I send you forth
to manifest energy for all the Earth.
Blessed be energy. *(Echo)*

I who am . . . Tell us and we will respond.

Greeting of Peace

Let us seal this commitment by sharing the peace of creation with
one another. *(Hugging)*

NOTES

1. "We Call upon the Earth, Our Planet Home," from *Chinook Blessing Litany*, in Roberts and Amidon, *Earth Prayers*, 106–07.

2. Betty Wendelborn, "We Are a Wheel," *Sing Green: Songs of the Mystics*, 2nd ed. (Auckland, New Zealand: Pyramid Press, 1999), 1.

3. Petra Kelly, *Thinking Green!* (Berkeley: Parallax Press, 1994), 7.

4. McFague, *Life Abundant*, 33.

5. "The Earth the Air, the Fire, the Water," from Libana, *A Circle Is Cast*.

6. Barbara Ward and Rene Dubos, *Only One Earth: The Care and Maintenance of a Small Planet* (New York: Norton, 1972), 220.

7. Williams, "Sin, Nature, and Black Women's Bodies," in Adams, *Ecofeminism and the Sacred*, 27–28.

8. Griffin, *Woman and Nature*, 219.

9. Anne Cameron, *Daughters of Copper Woman* (Vancouver: Press Gang Publishers, 1981), 44.

10. Hildegard of Bingen, "Glance at the Sun," in Uhlein, *Meditations with Hildegard of Bingen*, 45.

11. Alice Walker, "Everything Is a Human Being," in *Living by the Word* (New York: Harcourt, Brace, Jovanovich, 1988), 148, 151.

12. Joanna Macy, "We Hear You, Fellow-Creatures," in Roberts and Amidon, *Earth Prayers*, 280.

13. "O Great Spirit" is a traditional Native American chant by Adele Getty, recorded by On Wings of Song and Robert Gass, on *O Great Spirit* © 1989, Spring Hill Music. Audio recording.

six

WALK IN BEAUTY

T he beauty of the universe surrounds all of humanity, especially during midspring. May (November) festivals celebrate this fertility. In the north May Day, Beltane, May 1, the month of Mary, Mother of God, and May Queens honor those who bring forth life. The Earth is warming again and the sun grows stronger. Beauty exists for all creation to notice, delight in, and give praise to our Creator.

This liturgy gives praise for the beauty of the Earth. It invites participants to walk in beauty and to restore beauty to the Earth. The Earth needs our protection so that it can be beautiful beyond seven generations.

Preparation

Place a feather, candle, bowl of water, and plant on the central symbol table. Around them put a variety of symbols that represent the Earth's beauty (e.g., shells, rocks, flowers).

Naming the Circle

Welcome to this liturgy, "Walk in Beauty." All of life is bursting forth in beauty these days—crocuses, daffodils, tulips, cherry blossoms, flowering trees. Let us speak our names and describe something of the Earth that is beautiful to us. *(Naming)*

Song: "For the Beauty of the Earth," by F. S. Pierpont

For the beauty of the Earth, for the glory of the skies,
For the love which from our birth over and around us lies,
Source of All to you we raise this our hymn of grateful praise.[1]

Call to Gather

(Four different people standing at the four directions—east, south, west, and north—call participants to prayer. If appropriate and convenient, each caller interacts with the element named. The first caller faces east, blows a feather, and speaks.)

Spirit of the East,
Filled with the winds of the air cycle,
Breathing the universe in and out again,
Come, bring beauty to planet Earth.

(The next caller faces south and lights a candle.)

Spirit of the South,
Filled with the metabolism of the fire cycle,
Producing energy to warm cold bodies,
Come, bring beauty to planet Earth.

(The third caller faces west, takes water from a bowl, and sprinkles the gathered.)

Spirit of the West,
Filled with the flow of the water cycle,
Pouring moisture in and through and out of you,
Come, bring beauty to planet Earth.

(The fourth caller faces north and touches a plant.)

Spirit of the North,
Filled with the creation of the Earth cycle,
Producing food to feed hungry creatures,
Come, bring beauty to planet Earth.

Prayer of Thanksgiving
(All pray in unison:)
Holy Creator, Wisdom Sophia, we give you thanks and praise. You make all life holy and fill the universe with your goodness. Give us strength to understand and eyes to see all that you entrust to our care. Teach us to walk the soft Earth as relatives to all that live and inhabit your creation. We honor and praise You, now and forever. Amen. Blessed be. Let it be so.

Song: "Now I Walk in Beauty," traditional Navajo Indian
(Sing as a round.)
1. Now I walk in beauty,
2. Beauty is before me,
3. Beauty is behind me,
4. Above and below me.[2]

Reading: "Glance at the Sun," by Hildegard of Bingen
Listen to the words of Hildegard of Bingen:

"Glance at the sun.
See the moon and the stars.
Gaze at the beauty of earth's greeting.
Now,
think.

What delight
God gives
to humankind
with all these things."[3]

Hymn of Praise: "All Creatures of Our God," tune by Lasst Uns Erfreuen, 1623)

LEADER: Praise God, you holy ones . . .
    Praise Wisdom Sophia, all shining stars.

SUNG RESPONSE: All creatures of our loving God,
    Lift up your voice with praise and laud,
    Alleluia! Alleluia!
    You blazing sun with golden beam.
    You silver moon with softer gleam!
    O praise God! O praise God!
    Alleluia! Alleluia! Alleluia!

LEADER: Praise God, highest heavens . . .
    She established you forever and ever.

SUNG RESPONSE: You rushing wind, air, clouds, and rain,
    By which all creatures you sustain.
    Alleluia! Alleluia!
    You rising morn, in praise rejoice,
    You lights of evening, find a voice
    O praise God! O praise God!
    Alleluia! Alleluia! Alleluia!

LEADER: Praise Wisdom Sophia, all the Earth . . .
    Storm winds that fulfill God's word.

SUNG RESPONSE: You swirling water, flowing clear,
    Make music for your God to hear,

Alleluia! Alleluia!
You glowing fire who lights the night,
Providing warmth, enhancing sight . . .
O praise God! O praise God!
Alleluia! Alleluia! Alleluia!

LEADER: You mountains and all you hills . . .
You creeping things and flying birds.

SUNG RESPONSE: **Dear gentle Earth, who day by day**
Unfolds your blessings on our way,
Alleluia! Alleluia!
The flowers and fruit that in you grow,
Let them God's glory also show!
   O praise God! O praise God!
   Alleluia! Alleluia! Alleluia!

LEADER: Let God be praised by all the faithful ones,
By the women of (*name your group*), the people close to God.

SUNG RESPONSE: **Let all on Earth our Creator bless,**
And praise our God in holiness,
Alleluia! Alleluia! Alleluia![4]

Reflection

The Earth is full of beauty. We walk in beauty daily. What beauty
did you notice today? What beauty do you wish for this season?
How will you work to restore beauty to the Earth? (*Sharing*)

Blessing the Earth's Beauty

In front of us are beautiful gifts from the Earth. Take one with
which you have a kinship right now. Listen to the message the
symbol has for you. (*Pause*)

Let us bless these symbols of the Earth's beauty. (*Participants
offer blessings in their own words.*)

Greeting of Beauty

Filled with the beauty of the gifts of the Earth that we have
blessed and with the beauty of one another, let us offer one another a greeting of beauty by exchanging our symbols with one
another and saying, "You are beauty for our world."

Song: "Wings Unfurled," by Colleen Fulmer

> You are fashioned in my image. You are woman, radiant Glory.
> Spirit rising, wings unfurled; you are beauty for our world.

> I am fashioned in God's image. I am woman, radiant Glory.
> Spirit rising, wings unfurled; I am beauty for our world.

> We are fashioned in God's image. We are women,
>   radiant Glory.
> Spirit rising, wings unfurled; we are beauty for our world.[5]

Sending Forth

> Beautiful women, let us go forth to walk in beauty.
> May beauty be within us.
> May beauty be around us.
> May beauty be ours in eternal life.

> Let us open our circle.

NOTES

1. From Re-Imagining Community, *Bring the Feast: Songs from
the Re-Imagining Community* (Cleveland, OH: Pilgrim Press, 1998),
14.

2. Recorded on Libana's *Fire Within* © 1990. A lovely dance
goes with this song (page 14 of accompanying book): line up, with

your left hand on the shoulder of the person in front of you. Walk slowly, in time to the music, using your right hand in this manner:

"Now I walk in beauty"—walk slowly in time to the music

"Beauty is before me"—hand on shoulder of person in front

"Beauty is behind me"—hand on the hand on your left shoulder

"Above and below me"—circle hand above and below, then to your heart

3. Hildegard of Bingen, "Glance at the Sun," in Uhlein, *Meditations with Hildegard of Bingen*, 45.

4. "All Creatures of Our God," music by Lasst Uns Erfreuen, in *Everflowing Streams: Songs for Worship*, ed. Ruth Duck and Michael Bausch (Cleveland, OH: Pilgrim Press, 1981), 6. Adapted by Diann Neu.

5. From Fulmer, *Her Wings Unfurled*.

part two

SUMMER *energized by the sun*

To God belongs all that the heavens and earth contain.

—Koran 22:64

Water flows from high in the mountains.
Water runs deep in the Earth.
Miraculously, water comes to us,
and sustains all life.

—Tich Nhat Hanh

The Goddess in all her manifestations was a
symbol of the unity of all life in Nature. Her power
was in water and stone, in tomb and cave, in animals
and birds, snakes and fish, hills, trees, and flowers. . . .
The Goddess gradually retreated into the depths of
forests or onto mountaintops, where she remains to this
day in beliefs and fairy stories. Human alienation from
the vital roots of earthly life ensued, the results of which
are clear in our contemporary society. But the cycles
never stop turning, and now we find the Goddess
reemerging from the forests and mountains,
bringing us hope for the future, returning us to
our most ancient human roots.

—Marija Gimbutas,
The Language of the Goddess

Summer is the time of greatest intensity and mutual sharing of light, air, water, and earth. These elements center within the young plant and facilitate the maturing process, which will then await the further interior transformation of autumn ripening. Summer light reveals the miraculous truth that has flowered from the apparent death of the Earth. Summer air breathes the freedom of rising up, stretching out, and reaching beyond to change patterns. Summer water refreshes, soothes, and anoints the vulnerable parched body and earth. Summer earth tenderly supports the maturing of her secrets.

This is the season to be outdoors with the earth, the trees, the animals, the herbs, and the gardens. The spirits of playfulness and leisure shine on long, hot days. We touch the grass barefooted, taste the salt water of the sea, hear frogs and mosquitoes, smell suntan lotion, see fireflies, and feel the heat of the sun.

The ecofeminist liturgies in this section focus the themes of solar power, leisure, activity, fullness, growth, and healing. They use the symbols of candles, bonfires, flames, starlight, sunlight, crystals, sand castles, travel maps, summer fruits and nuts, soil, and seedlings. They urge us to heal the Earth in summer by taking a walk around the neighborhood and picking up trash, wearing cotton clothes, watering the garden, setting up a recycle craft box for children, buying foods from local farmers, choosing reusable cloth napkins instead of paper ones, and recycling paper, glass, plastic, and aluminum. Use them as models to celebrate the summer festivals of June 21 (December 21), summer solstice, and of August 1 (February 1), Lammas, the first harvest.

seven

SUMMER SOLSTICE AS PRAISE THE SUN

The summer solstice, on about June 21 (December 21), is the absolute peak of solar power. The sun is at its apex while at its turning point. The sun is in its farthest position away from the equator, and the hemisphere on which it shines is receiving the fullest force of light and energy. At the pole solar energy abounds around the clock. This is the longest day and shortest night of the year. It signals that changes in light and weather are coming. Nature is at the summit of its sumptuousness, as light and as ripe as it can possibly get. Summer solstice festivals celebrate the sun and renew the community's ties to the Earth.

This liturgy is most freeing when celebrated outside, but can also be effective inside. It invites participants to feel the rainbow of colors from the sun, to share the fulfillment, passion, and creativity they wish for themselves and for the Earth.

Preparation

Alert participants to wake up at sunrise. Create the symbol space by placing a bonfire (grill) in the center of the yard. Have a basket of twigs, seven candles, drinks, and ingredients for s'mores ("some mores"): marshmallows, chocolate squares, and graham crackers. Gather musical instruments (drums, rattles, tambourines) for the participants.

Salute to the Sun

(One who knows dance or yoga begins the liturgy by walking to the center of the circle, lighting a candle, and saluting the sun using body gestures in keeping with these words, and motioning all to follow suit.)

Face the sun. *(Pause)* Stand united with the warm Earth. *(Pause)* Lift your arms to the sun. *(Pause)* Feel the energy flow through your hands and arms. *(Pause)* Pull the sun's energy toward your eyes. *(Pause)* Hug yourself passionately. *(Pause)* Feel the energy flow through your body and your feet. *(Pause)* Connect with the sun and the Earth.

Naming the Circle

Welcome to this celebration of the summer solstice. This longest day and shortest night of the year remind us that summer is here. To create our circle, speak your name, your community affiliations, and say, "I honor the sun and you." *(Sharing. If it is raining, incorporate this by inviting people to say, "I honor the rain, the sun, and you.")*

Song: "Over My Head," traditional African American spiritual, adapted

> Over my head I see summer in the air,
> Over my head I see summer in the air,
> Over my head I see summer in the air,
> There must be a God somewhere.
>
> Over my head I see freedom in the air . . .

(Repeat, using the following for each new verse.) . . . sunshine . . . passion . . . dancing . . . renewal . . . energy . . . abundance . . . fulfillment

Call to Gather

(One leader lights the fire while another says:)

Happy Midsummer to you! This date is known as Midsummer's Night, the longest day and the shortest night of the year. On this night the Earth reaches midpoint on its journey around the sun. This is a night of fulfillment. It is a magical time when wishes are made and come true. The Earth is transparent and its underground riches can be seen. It is a significant turning point in the Wheel of the Year.

In ancient agricultural rites, fires were lit at summer solstice to renew the sun's energy while it was at its turning point. Indigenous Europeans built sun shrines. Stonehenge, a famous stone circle, has its main axis in perfect alignment with the summer solstice sunrise. The Aztecs, Mayans, and Incas of Central America, the Chinese, and the Egyptians all built sun shrines. In many Native American traditions, this time of year is celebrated as part of a vision cycle, and dances are performed to renew the energy of the sun, the vegetation, and the people. On this day the Hopi Indians of the Southwest celebrate Niman Kachina when the kachinas, the tribal spirit guides, return to their underground homes until the winter solstice.

In Brazil, people set flower wreaths on fire and float them on the waves to honor the Yoruba sea goddess, Iamanja. In Christian tradition, summer solstice, or St. John's Eve, marks the birth of John the Baptist, who told of the coming of Christ the Light. Even today, St. John's fires are lit in the mountains of Europe. The flames of sun and fire remind us of the early Christian community's Pentecost experience of empowerment by the Spirit. In the goddess tradition, summer solstice was known as Litha, the name of a northern European and North African goddess of fertility, power, and abundance.

In many lands, the ancestors designed and built solar observatories for the summer solstice that are in perfect alignment with the sun's path on this date. These marvels of astronomy were created as medicine wheels in caves and in such places as Stonehenge, Casa Grande, Woodhenge, and New Grange.

In feminist circles around the world, the summer solstice is being welcomed as a time to renew passions, to give thanks for the abundant gifts of the Earth, and to promise to protect all things under the sun.

Red and yellow are the colors for summer solstice: the red of passion, the yellow of the sun, and the red of the summer bonfire. Red and yellow flowers enhance our celebration. This day may our wishes be fulfilled!

Invoking the Goddesses of Fire

(Two readers introduce the litany, name several goddesses, and throw twigs on the fire or light a candle in their honor.)

Chant: "Rise Up, O Flame," by Pretorius

Rise up, O flame, by thy light glowing
Show to us beauty, vision, and joy.[1]

READER ONE: Let us call upon the female divinities, the goddesses of fire, to be with us this summer solstice.

Goddesses of Fire,
Sparking, glowing, searing powers,
Strong Ones who dance,
Passionate Ones who move the ever-turning wheel of creation,
We welcome you.

ALL: Rise up, O flame, by thy light glowing
Show to us beauty, vision, and joy.

READER TWO: Hail, Mawu of Dahomey, goddess of earth and fire. Be with us.

Hail, Akewa of Argentina, goddess of air and fire. Be with us.
Hail, Pele of Polynesia, goddess of passion and fire. Be with us.
(The reader lights a candle or throws twigs on the fire.)

ALL: Rise up, O flame, by thy light glowing
Show to us beauty, vision, and joy.

READER ONE: Hail, Oshun of West Africa, goddess of water
and fire. Be with us.
    Hail, Sun Woman of Australia, goddess of immortality and
spirit. Be with us.
    Hail, Gaia, mother goddess of the Greeks. Be with us.
(*The reader lights a candle or throws twigs on the fire.*)

ALL: Rise up, O flame, by thy light glowing
Show to us beauty, vision, and joy.

READER TWO: Hail, Tiamat, brave warrior of the Semites, from
whose broken body the world was made. Be with us.
    Hail, Ishtar and Asherah, long sacred to the Mesopotamians
and Hebrews. Be with us.
    Hail, Inanna, beloved of Sumeria, who dared to journey to
the underworld for your sister's sake. Be with us.
(*The reader lights a candle or throws twigs on the fire.*)

ALL: Rise up, O flame, by thy light glowing
Show to us beauty, vision, and joy.

READER ONE: Hail, Spider Woman, goddess of the native peoples of the American Southwest. Be with us.
    Hail, Amaterasu, sacred to the ancient people of Japan. Be
with us.
    Hail, Yemaya, river mother of West Africa. Be with us.
    Hail, Rhiannon, goddess of the Welsh, horse-rider and bird-
singer. Be with us.
(*The reader lights a candle or throws twigs on the fire.*)

ALL: Rise up, O flame, by thy light glowing
Show to us beauty, vision, and joy.

Meditation on Summer Solstice

(Three guides lead the following meditation:)

GUIDE ONE: Bonfire light, candlelight, and sunlight reflect the power of fire. Feel the rainbow of colors in the flames as we meditate on the summer solstice. *(Pause)*

Make your body comfortable to feel the movement and heartbeat of the Earth at this solstice time.

Feel the richness of Mother Earth as she shares her summer colors with you. Draw these colors into your body, through your feet, legs, genitals, abdomen, heart, chest, hands, arms, throat, and head. Feel the treasures of the summer solstice.

GUIDE TWO: Feel the color red, the longest wavelength, the flow of life in your blood, the color of courage. Be attentive to your courage.

GUIDE THREE: Feel the vibrant orange, the action color, the primary ray connected to the womb center, the color of passion. Be attentive to your passion.

GUIDE ONE: Feel the opening yellow, the expanding wavelength, the color of transcendence, the color of will. Be attentive to your openness.

GUIDE TWO: Feel the growing green, the middle of the spectrum, the color of sympathy and emotion, the color of balance. Be attentive to your growth.

GUIDE THREE: Feel the calming blue, the creative color, the color of the sky, the power of decision making. Be attentive to your calm.

GUIDE ONE: Feel the wise indigo, the passive wavelength, the color of psychic knowing, the color of awareness. Be attentive to your intuition.

GUIDE TWO: Feel the compassion of purple, the shortest wavelength, the color of the older woman, the color of introspection and spiritual development. Be attentive to your spirituality.

GUIDE THREE: Feel the earthiness of brown, the stable color, the color of security, the color of centering. Be attentive to your center.

GUIDE ONE: Draw in what you need and want from these solstice colors. Draw in fulfillment, passion, and abundance from the gifts of Mother Earth, and release them to the universe as they manifest themselves to you. Spend some time with this kaleidoscope of colors and their gifts. *(Pause)*

GUIDE TWO: Slowly, feel the colors stop. Invite a wish to emerge out of this color rainbow. *(Pause)* Know all colors are within you. Focus on the bonfire. *(Pause)* Know all wishes will be granted. *(Pause)* Come back to now. *(Pause)*

Reflection

GUIDE THREE: Focus on the sun, the candles, and the fire. Feel the rainbow of colors in the flames. You are a flame filled with this rainbow of colors. What peaks of energy do you experience? What fulfillment, passion, and creativity do you wish for yourself and for the Earth this solstice? *(Pause)* Share a glimpse of this and, if you choose, speak your wish and throw a twig or herbs on the fire to carry your wish home to the Cosmic Mother as a message. Or, if you prefer, just throw a twig or herbs on the fire in silence. *(Sharing)*

Song: "Walk Into the Holy Fire," author unknown

> Walk into the holy fire, step into the holy flame,
> Walk into the holy fire, step into the holy flame.
> Aleluya. Aleluya.[2]

Remembering Those Who Need Healing

There are many who need our prayers this day. Let us speak the needs and answer with a sentence you would like us to repeat, such as "May the warm sun heal you."

Song: "Fire Song," by Starhawk

(Clap, use drums, rattles, and percussion instruments.)

We can rise with the fire of freedom;
truth is a fire that burns our chains,
And we can stop the fire of destruction;
healing is a fire running through our veins.[3]

Taking the Solstice Leap

We bring closure to our solstice time by taking a summer solstice leap! It is traditional on this day to leap over the fire. Those who wish can leap over the candles. For protection in the coming year, for the courage to take risks, for purification from sorrow, and for the fun of feeling foolish again, jump over the fire. Now take another leap for the protection of all things under the sun and on the Earth this millennium. *(Leaping)*

Song and Spiral Dance: "Dancing Sophia's Circle," by Colleen Fulmer

Ring us round, O blazing circle,
Great Mother dancing free,
Beauty, strength, and Holy Wisdom,
Blessing you and blessing me.[4]

Sending Forth

Let us go forth conscious of the sun's position throughout
the rest of today.
Let us honor today's sunset with our complete attention.
And after sunset, let us burn candles or fires as our ancestors
did to energize the sun as it begins to turn toward darkness.

Eating

Bonfires remind me of toasting marshmallows and eating s'mores. Let us have fun as we prepare for the solstice. Come, toast a

marshmallow, put it on a graham cracker with a piece of chocolate, and make a delicious sandwich like children do.

Closing

Tomorrow, wake up again at sunrise. Commune with the rising
sun. Remain conscious of the sun throughout the day and honor
the sunset with your complete attention. After sunset, forgo electric lights. Burn candles or a bonfire, as the ancients did, to feed
the sun as it turns to darkness. Enjoy the summer solstice. Let us
open our circle.

NOTES

1. Round recorded on *Fire Within*, by Libana.

2. "Walk Into the Holy Fire," reprinted from Middleton, *Songs
for Earthlings*, 32.

3. Starhawk, "Fire Song," reprinted from Middleton, *Songs for
Earthlings*, 33.

4. Colleen Fulmer, "Dancing Sophia's Circle," *Dancing Sophia's
Circle* ©1994, Heartbeats. Audio recording.

PRAYER OF DIRECTIONS

The Prayer of the Directions has roots in matriarchal cultures and in indigenous traditions. It blesses creation and can be prayed as the Prayer of the Four, Five, Six, or Seven Directions. The Prayer of the Four Directions refers to north, east, south, and west. The Fifth Direction is center. The Prayer of Six Directions uses north, east, south, west, above, and below. The Prayer of the Seven Directions is given here.

The proper place for this prayer is outside, but it can be done inside, preferably in a space with windows. Face the north to start, or begin with the direction that is an appropriate one for your group, given the season, time of day, or geographic location. As you pray, turn in a circle to face the direction of your prayer. When using this prayer, invite a different person to lead each part or have two people share the readings and pray the center direction together. It is very powerful to give people the idea of the directions and ask them to create their own prayers.

A word of caution: Apply these directions to your own country. The seasons and other specifics (i.e., animals, plants, climate) for the directions may vary.

This prayer has been adapted and readapted by groups all over the world. It is a blessing prayer that can welcome or close a day or a meeting. It can be used within a liturgy as an invocation of the Great Spirits. It can also be used for personal reflection or individual prayer.

Invocation of the Spirits

(Face north. Cross your arms in front of your chest and sway from side to side.)

O Great Spirit of the North, we come to you and ask for the strength and the power to bear what is cold and harsh in life. We come ready to receive the winds that truly can be overwhelming at times. Whatever is cold and uncertain in our lives, we ask you to give us the strength to bear it. Do not let the winter blow us away. Do not let that which seems to ask us to wait for life be lost in mystery. O Spirit of Life and Spirit of the North, we ask you for strength and for warmth.

(Take a deep breath, drop your arms to your sides, face east, raise your arms above your head.)

O Great Spirit of the East, we turn to you where the sun comes up, from where the power of light and refreshment come. Everything that is born comes up in this direction—the birth of babies, the birth of puppies, the birth of ideas, and the birth of friendship. Let there be light. O Spirit of the East, let the color of fresh rising in our lives be glory to you.

(Take a deep breath, drop your arms to your sides, face south, put your arms around one another and sway.)

O Great Spirit of the South, spirit of all that is warm and gentle and refreshing, we ask you to give us this spirit of growth, of fertility, of gentleness. Caress us with a cool breeze when the days are hot. Give us seeds that the flowers, trees, and fruits of the Earth may grow. We love the grass and the trees and the flowers; we love the land. Give us the warmth of good friendships. O Spirit of the South, send the warmth, growth, and fruition of your blessings.

(Take a deep breath, drop your arms to your sides, face west, extend your arms outward, palms up, in a gesture of receiving.)

O Great Spirit of the West, where the sun goes down each day to come up the next, we turn to you in praise of sunsets and in thanksgiving for changes. You are the great colored sunset of the red that illuminates us. You are the powerful cycle that pulls us to transformation. We ask for the blessings of the sunset. Keep us open to life's changes. O Spirit of the West, when it is time for us to go to rest, do not desert us, but receive us in the arms of our loved ones.

(Take a deep breath, breathe yourself up, face up, raise your whole body up, stretch your head up, spread your arms.)

O Great Spirit of All That Is Above, of everything that soars, of all that flies, of all high visions, all that is above the Earth, we honor you and glorify you for the power that you are. Lift our minds and our hearts above the Earth so that we may never be afraid of great heights and of looking like the eagle high across the land. O Spirit of All That Is Above, put us on the wings of spirit travel so that we may know this world.

(Take a deep breath, breathe your arms to your sides, face down, and bend over from the waist.)

O Great Spirit of All That Is Below, of all that pulls us to deeper places, to the depths of ourselves, we turn to you in the memory of all that goes down. We ask you to give us the strength and the courage to face death. When people leave us in this life to share life with you, let there not be a grief that is untrue. When we experience losses and changes in our lives, let us see them as your revelation. O Spirit of All That Is Below, purify us.

(Take a deep breath, breathe your body to center, face center, extend your hands, palms outward to rest in the palms of the persons on either side of you.)

O Great Spirit of Everything That Is Center, of everything that is free, we come to you with gratitude. We thank you and bless you for being with us, for calling us to be centered within ourselves. Remind us that it is only from this center that we reach out to others. Breathe through us that your work of justice may be done. O Great Spirit of everything of the heart and everything that is mystery, send us forth to walk a way of beauty and holiness. Open our hearts to friendship. O Spirit of Everything That Is Center, never let us forget that you are the center of hope.

(Drop your hands and embrace one another in peace.)

nine

A GARDEN OF ABUNDANCE

The first harvest of the year is celebrated in August (February) when fruits and vegetables are plentiful. During this month of fulfillment and abundance we celebrate festivals of the first fruits of the harvest. Lammas, the Celtic festival of the new bread, commemorates rebirth by reaping spring wheat. The Green Corn Ceremony of the Creek Native Americans gives thanks for a plentiful garden and asks the gods for continued prosperity. Picnics and county fairs mark the bounty and wealth of the Earth. These festivals celebrate the ripening gifts of wheat, corn, vegetables, and grapes.

This liturgy focuses on the abundance of the garden, the awareness of life's richness. It invites participants to notice areas of plenty in their lives and reflect on the harvest they will store up for the winter.

Preparation

Place symbols of the garden's bounty—wheat, corn, tomatoes, zucchini, eggplant, basil, mint, grapes, bread, cider, and wine—in the center of the circle. Surround them with candles, one for each participant.

Naming the Circle

This is the beginning of the fruitful season. Tonight we celebrate the first harvest of the year, "A Garden of Abundance." Let us introduce ourselves in this circle by saying our names, passing an ear of corn, and sharing thoughts we have about abundance. (*Sharing*)

Call to Gather

Today we honor abundance, just as generations before us did and, we hope, those after us will. Festivals of prosperity mark this season. Lammas, the Celtic festival of the new bread, honored the grain that is the staple of life. The Creek Native Americans celebrate the Green Corn Ceremony to give thanks for their plentiful harvest and ask the gods for continued prosperity. In our society markets are full of the abundance of this first harvest of the year. Farmers' markets are plentiful. County fairs compete for the largest zucchini and best apple pie. In each culture this season marks the prosperity and wealth of the Earth. Let us center ourselves to celebrate the abundance we reap from our gardens.

Song: "Song of Community," by Carolyn McDade

> We'll weave a love that greens sure as spring,
> Then deepens in summer to the fall autumn brings
> Resting still in winter to spiral again
> Together my friends we'll weave on, we'll weave on.

Chorus:
> A love that heals, friend, that bends, friend,
> That rising and turning then yields, friend,

Like mountain to rain or frost in the spring
Or darkness that turns with the dawn.
It's by turning, turning, turning, my friend,
By turning that love moves on.

We'll weave a love with roots growing deep
And sap pushing branches to wake from their sleep
Bearing leaves burnt amber with morning's full sweep.
Together, my friends, we'll weave on, we'll weave on.

(Chorus)[1]

Reading: "The Garden Is Rich with Diversity," in the *Chinook Psalter*

The garden is rich with diversity
With plants of a hundred families
In the space between the trees
With all the colors and fragrances.
Basil, mint, and lavender,
God, keep my remembrance pure.
Raspberry, apple, rose,
God, fill my heart with love.
Dill, anise, tansy,
Holy winds, blow in me.
Rhododendron, zinnia,
May my prayer be beautiful.
May my remembrance, O God,
Be as incense to thee
In the sacred grove of eternity
As I smell and remember
The ancient forests of Earth.[2]

Lighting the Candles

As the nights grew longer, the Druids, priests of the Celtic people
of Ireland and the British Isles, feared that the sun might cease to

shine, leaving the Earth to the forces of evil. They believed fire reenergized the sun and drove away evil spirits.

Let us bring the energy of our abundance into this room by lighting candles. (*Each participant lights a candle.*)

Meditation on Harvest

Let us be quiet with ourselves to attune ourselves to a garden of abundance. (*Pause*)

Let the sacred period of late summer teach us the virtues of contentment and at-homeness with its multicolored riches. Let it teach us to take stock of what we have given and received, to know that these are enough. May it open us to delight in the abundance of life.

So often scarcity, or the fear of scarcity, captures our attention and takes our energy. Abundance is a presence that supports and nurtures us without demands. It is an awareness of life's riches. Take time to notice areas of abundance in your life: your health, your chosen family and friends, your training and experience, your home, and your relationship with the Earth and the stars. (*Pause*)

What abundance do you have in your life and how are you returning blessing to all creation from what you have received? Let us take time for three minutes of quiet reflection and then we will share our thoughts. (*Reflection*)

Let us share with one another a glimpse of our reflections. What abundance do you have in your life and how are you returning blessing to all creation from what you have received? (*Sharing*)

Blessing an Abundant Garden

There are many symbols of plenty here. Pick up one that is near you so that we may bless this abundance. (*Participants pick up the symbols. One prays.*)

Let us extend our hands over these symbols:

Blessed are you, Sustainer of All. We thank you for the gifts of an abundant garden. They are symbols of our creative energy, the energy and newness of spring, which deepens and matures in late summer. We thank you for the strength and the labor of women we have known: farmers, gardeners, homemakers, office workers, and all who labor, women whose muscle and mind move our world and speak of the power of women.

Let us bless these symbols by remembering women who sweat and toil for liberation and equality. Let us speak their names. (*Sharing*)

Song: "Something about the Women," by Holly Near

Oh, there's something about the women,
There's something about the women,
Something about the women in my life. (*Repeat*)[3]

Blessing the Apple

(*The person with the apple prays:*)
Blessed are you, Creator of All. We thank you for the apples we share. They are the fruit of the early harvest, symbol of the fullness and ripeness of mature orchards, emblematic of women's knowledge. We thank you for the ripe, wise women we have known: middle-aged women, hags and crones, women who speak out in wisdom against all that holds us back from fullness.

Let us bless these apples by remembering the names of the wise women in our lives: our mothers, grandmothers, wise ones who birth, nurture, guide, and love us. Let us speak their names. (*Sharing*)

Song

Oh, there's something about the women,
There's something about the women,
Something about the women in my life. (*Repeat*)

Blessing the Bread

(The person with the bread prays:)

Blessed are you, Sustenance of All Life. We give you thanks for the bread we take, bless, break, and eat. It comes from the fruits of our labors, symbol of the fullness and ripeness of late summer. We thank you for the diversity and power of women: women of all colors and shapes, women from different countries who speak a variety of languages, all beautiful women with abundant gifts.

Let us bless this bread by remembering women who bake bread, breastfeed children, prepare meals, and feed hungry souls. Let us speak their names. *(Sharing)*

Song

Oh, there's something about the women,
There's something about the women,
Something about the women in my life. *(Repeat)*

Blessing the Fruit of the Vine

(The persons with the glasses of cider and wine raise them and one prays:)

Blessed are you, Lover of All. We thank you for the wine and juice we toast with and share. They come from the fruits of summer, a symbol of the joy and warmth of this season. We thank you for the passion and joy of women we have known: young women, women-children and adolescents, women who celebrate all that yearns for completion.

Let us bless these drinks by remembering our friends, daughters, nieces, teachers, and students, who share their passion for life with the world. Let us speak their names. *(Sharing)*

Communion

Let us share these vegetables and bread, this juice and wine, remembering our harvest. *(Eating and drinking)*

Song

> Oh, there's something about the women,
> There's something about the women,
> Something about the women in my life. *(Repeat)*

Blessing One Another

Let us put our arms around one another as we pray:

Blessed are you, Mother of All. We thank you for our selves, the greatest gifts we share with one another. We are the symbols of your warmth, caring, power, and wisdom.

We thank you for all the people who have touched our lives and revealed you to us: those who listen to us, who hear us, who counsel us, who heal us, people whose concern and support call us to an abundant harvest.

Let us bless one another by remembering friends who see visions of what can be and share that with us: seers, activists, creative spirits. Let us speak their names. *(Sharing)*

Sending Forth

And let us embrace one another and send one another forth with a greeting of shared bounty. *(Hugging)*

Song: "The Circle Is Open," author unknown

> The circle is open yet unbroken,
> May the peace of the Goddess go ever in your heart.
> Merry meet, and merry part and merry meet again.[4]

NOTES

1. From McDade, *Rain Upon Dry Land*, 8.
2. In Roberts and Amidon, *Earth Prayers*, 309.

3. Holly Near (words and music), "Something about the Women," *Imagine My Surprise!* © 1978, Hereford Music (ASCAP). Audio recording.

4. Reprinted from Middleton, *Songs for Earthlings*, 142.

ten

THE EARTH IS SACRED

All creatures share an interconnection with planet Earth, the sustainer of life. We are each called to care for this sacred planet of our birth and growth. We must treasure her beauty and protect her from abuse. The Earth is sacred.

This liturgy begins by inviting participants to acknowledge that "we have forgotten who we are." To reconnect with the Earth, the gathered lie down under a tree for a guided meditation. To show love and care for the Earth, they are invited to rid the world of destructive patterns, accept the rhythms of life and death, and become cocreators. They pull weeds, compost, and plant seedlings.

Preparation

Gather outside beneath a tree and invite participants to sit on the ground. In the center, or around the tree, place a globe, a bucket of soil, seedlings, garden tools, and a basket of apples.

Naming the Circle

The Earth is sacred and we must care for her. Let us create our circle by taking the globe, speaking our names, and saying, "I will take care of the Earth." *(Naming)*

Call to Gather

We have just promised to take care of the Earth. That is a lifetime commitment. The Earth is sacred. She is a precious space of ever-greening life and ever-changing beauty. We all live on her. How are we taking care of planet Earth? How do we tread upon her ground? Let us gather, singing a nursery rhyme with new words, remembering we have lived on this Earth since our birth.

Song: "Ever Greening Mother Earth," by Irene Lucas, tune "Twinkle, Twinkle, Little Star"

> Ever greening Mother Earth,
> You have held us from our birth.
> You have hugged the birds and trees
> In your hands, the fish and seas.
> Ever greening Mother Earth,
> You have held us from our birth.
>
> Ever greening Mother Earth,
> You have held all from their birth.
> You have loved the young and old,
> The rich, the poor, the weak, the bold.
> Ever greening Mother Earth,
> You have held all from their birth.

Ever spinning Planet Dear,
We have filled our home with fear.
We have fashioned guns and swords.
We have played at games of war.
Ever spinning Planet Dear,
We have filled our home with fear.

Ever spinning Planet Dear,
Don't be sad; your kids are here.
We don't like what grownups do.
We want to say that we love you.
Ever spinning Planet Dear,
Don't be sad; your kids are here.

Ever greening Mother Earth,
You have held us from our birth.[1]

Reading: "We Have Forgotten Who We Are," United Nations Environmental Sabbath Program

LEADER: We have forgotten who we are. Let us say this each time I gesture with my hand. (*Gesture*)

RESPONSE: **We have forgotten who we are.**

LEADER: We have forgotten who we are.
We have alienated ourselves from the unfolding of the cosmos.
We have become estranged from the movements of the Earth.
We have turned our backs on the cycles of life.

RESPONSE: **We have forgotten who we are.**

LEADER: We have sought only our own security.
We have exploited simply for our own ends.
We have distorted our knowledge.
We have abused our power.

RESPONSE: **We have forgotten who we are.**

LEADER: Now the land is barren
 And the waters are poisoned
 And the air is polluted.

RESPONSE: **We have forgotten who we are.**

LEADER: Now the forests are dying
 And the creatures are disappearing
 And humans are despairing.

RESPONSE: **We have forgotten who we are.**

LEADER: We ask forgiveness.
 We ask for the gift of remembering.
 We ask for the strength to change.

RESPONSE: **We have forgotten who we are.**[2]

Reading: "What Are You? What Am I?" by John Seed and
Joanna Macy

What are you? What am I? Intersecting cycles of water, earth, air,
and fire, that's what I am, that's what you are.

Water—blood, lymph, mucus, sweat, tears, inner oceans
tugged by the moon, tides within and tides without. Streaming
fluids floating our cells, washing and nourishing through endless
river ways of gut and vein and capillary. Moisture spouting in and
through and out of you, of me, in the vast poem of the hydrolog-
ical cycle. You are that, I am that.

Earth—matter made from rock and soil. The moon too pulls
it as the magma circulates through the planet heart, and roots
suck molecules into biology. Earth pours through us, replacing
each cell in the body every seven years. Ashes to ashes, dust to
dust, we ingest, incorporate, and excrete the earth, are made from
the earth. I am that. You are that.

Air—the gaseous realm, the atmosphere, the planet's mem-
brane. The inhale and the exhale. Breathing out carbon dioxide to
the trees and breathing in their fresh exudations. Oxygen kissing

each cell awake, atoms dancing in orderly metabolism, interpenetrating. That dance of the air cycle, breathing the universe in and out again, is what you are, is what I am.

Fire—fire from our sun that fuels all life, drawing up plants and raising the waters to the sky to fall again replenishing. The inner furnace of your metabolism burns with the fire of the Big Bang that first sent matter-energy spinning through space and time. And the same fire as the lightning that flashed into the primordial soup catalyzing the birth of organic life.

You were there, I was there, for each cell of our bodies is descended in an unbroken chain from that event.[3]

Chant: "Earth My Body," author unknown

Earth my body, water my blood, air my breath, and fire my spirit. (*Sing three times*)[4]

Meditation

Lie down under the tree. Rest on the ground and get in touch with the Earth as a living process—the humus, the organic matter in the soil. Picture the roots of the tree reaching down into the Earth, drawing up water and minerals to the branches. Image the sap rising through the trunk, reaching out along the branches. Hear the leaves drawing in the sunlight, transforming the carbon dioxide into oxygen. Think about your own body, the many ways in which it is interconnected with the Earth. Feel the connection. (*Pause*)

Chant

Earth my body, water my blood, air my breath, and fire my spirit. (*Sing three times*)

Reading: "The Earth Is Mother," by Hildegard of Bingen

The Earth is at the same time
Mother,

She is mother of all that is natural,
   Mother of all that is human

She is the mother of all,
For contained in her
Are the seeds of all.

The Earth of humankind
Contains all moistness,
   All verdancy,
     All germinating power.

It is in so many ways
Fruitful.
All creation comes from it.[5]

CMeditation

Sit up, slowly. Feel connected to the Earth. Touch the grass and the soil. Go into the Earth.

Chant

Earth my body, water my blood, air my breath, and fire my spirit. (*Sing three times*)

Reading: "The Earth: What She Is to Me," by Susan Griffin

As I go into the Earth, she pierces my heart. As I penetrate further, she unveils me. When I have reached her center, I am weeping openly. I have known her all my life, yet she reveals stories to me, and these stories are revelations and I am transformed. Each time I go to her I am born like this. Her renewal washes over me endlessly, her wounds caress me; I become aware of all that has come between us, of the noise between us, the blindness, of something sleeping between us. Now my body reaches out to her. They speak effortlessly, and I learn at no instant does she fail me in her presence. She is as delicate as I am; I know her sentience; I feel her pain and my own pain comes into me, and my open pain grows large and I grasp this pain with my hands, and I open my mouth to this pain, I taste, I know, and I know why she goes on, under great weight, with this great thirst, in drought, in starvation, with intelligence in every act does she survive disaster. This Earth is my sister; I love her daily grace, her silent daring, and how loved I am, how we admire this strength in each other, all that we have lost, all that we have suffered, all that we know: we are stunned by this beauty, and I do not forget: what she is to me, what I am to her.[6]

Meditation

Stand up, slowly. How do you experience a connection to the pain and the power of the Earth? Let us share with one another our thoughts and feelings. (*Sharing*)

Song: "The Earth Is Our Mother," author unknown, additional verses by Morning Glory Zell

(*The dance step is step right with right foot, close step with left foot. Repeat and continue moving in a circle to the right.*)

    The Earth is our Mother, we must take care of her,
    The Earth is our Mother, we must take care of her.
    Hey yana ho yana hey yan yan,
    Hey yana ho yana hey yan yan.

    Her sacred ground we walk upon, with every step we take
        (*Repeat*)
    Hey yana ho yana hey yan yan, (*Repeat*)

    The fire that can warm us, is in the love we make (*Repeat*)
    Hey yana ho yana hey yan yan, (*Repeat*)

    The air we breathe renews us, with every breath we take
        (*Repeat*)
    Hey yana ho yana hey yan yan, (*Repeat*)

From water that we drink of, comes all the life she makes
   (*Repeat*)
Hey yana ho yana hey yan yan, (*Repeat*)[7]

Reading: "Be a Gardener," by Julian of Norwich

Be a gardener.
Dig and ditch,
toil and sweat,
and turn the Earth upside down
and seek the deepness
and water the plants in time.
Continue this labor
and make sweet floods to run
and noble and abundant fruits
to spring.
Take this food and drink
and carry it to God
as your true worship.[8]

Reflection

To love and care for the Earth we must do three things. One, rid the world of destructive patterns. Two, accept the rhythms of death and life. Three, celebrate the beauty of the world and enter into the process of cocreation.

So we ask you to do these three things now. First, get up and pull a noxious weed. Second, put the weed into the compost. And third, plant a seedling. (*Weeding and planting*)

(*Regroup in a circle in the grass for sharing.*)

Let us share our experience with one another. How am I caring for planet Earth? (*Sharing*)

Litany of Praise

LEADER: Let us close our sharing with a litany of praise. Respond with, "Praise Our Creator."

Let the Earth praise God.

RESPONSE: **Praise Our Creator.**

LEADER: Praise the Source of Life, all creation.

RESPONSE: **Praise Our Creator.**

LEADER: Sing praise to the Holy One forever.

RESPONSE: **Praise Our Creator.**

LEADER: Skies above and waters below,

RESPONSE: **Praise Our Creator.**

LEADER: Sun, moon, stars, and planets,

RESPONSE: **Praise Our Creator.**

LEADER: Rain and dew, winds and breezes,

RESPONSE: **Praise Our Creator.**

LEADER: Fire and heat, ice and cold,

RESPONSE: **Praise Our Creator.**

LEADER: Green plants and ancient forests,

RESPONSE: **Praise Our Creator.**

LEADER: Birds of the air and fish of the sea,

RESPONSE: **Praise Our Creator.**

LEADER: Nights and days, years and centuries,

RESPONSE: **Praise Our Creator.**

LEADER: Frost and snow, lightning and thunder,

RESPONSE: **Praise Our Creator.**

LEADER: Mountains and hills, lakes and rivers,

RESPONSE: **Praise Our Creator.**

LEADER: Winged, multilegged, four-legged and two-legged creatures,

RESPONSE: **Praise Our Creator.**

Blessing the Apple

(One person takes the basket of apples and prays:)

Blessed are you, Creator of All. We thank you for the apples we share. They are the fruit of the early harvest, symbol of the fullness and ripeness of mature orchards, emblematic of women's knowledge. We thank you for the ripe, wise women we have known: middle-aged women, hags and crones, women who speak out in wisdom against all that holds us back from fullness.

Let us bless these apples by remembering the names of the wise women in our lives: our mothers, grandmothers, wise ones who birth, nurture, guide, and love us. Let us speak their names and tell their stories as we eat these apples. *(Eating and sharing)*

Sending Forth

Filled with the fruits of summer and connected to the sacredness of the Earth, let us open our circle and go forth gently.

Song: "Touch the Earth," by Kathy Sherman

Refrain: Touch the Earth with gentleness,
Touch the Earth with love.
Touch her with a future by the way you live today.
God has given us the power to create the world anew
We touch the Earth together, me and you.

Time is here, the time is now; we can change things.
Give the Earth your dream, for harmony she is waiting;
Waiting for love, waiting for you, waiting for me.

(Refrain)

Show the Earth you care about her future,
Melt the walls of hate and fear that keep us apart.
Believe we can live together as friends on Earth.

(Refrain)

Be the reason, be the hope for others to believe
That the Earth is meant for beauty, goodness, and peace,
And that our God of love is God of the Earth's one family.

(Refrain)[9]

NOTES

1. In *Pax Christi USA*, 5, no. 4 (Winter 1991), 23.

2. In Roberts and Amidon, *Earth Prayers*, 70–71.

3. In John Seed and Joanna Macy, *Thinking Like a Mountain: Toward a Council of All Beings* (Stony Creek, CT: New Society Publishers, 1988), 280.

4. Reprinted from Middleton, *Songs for Earthlings*, 116.

5. In Uhlein, *Meditations of Hildegard of Bingen*, 58.

6. In Griffin, *Woman and Nature*, 219.

7. "The Earth Is Our Mother," author unknown, additional verses by Morning Glory Zell, reprinted from Middleton, *Songs for Earthlings*, 23.

8. In Brendan Doyle, ed., *Meditations with Julian of Norwich* (Santa Fe, NM: Bear & Co., 1983), 84.

9. "Touch the Earth" by Kathy Sherman, CSJ, from *Touch the Earth* © 1987. Courtesy of the Ministry of the Arts, Sisters of St. Joseph, LaGrange, IL. www.ministryofthearts.org. Audio recording.

part three

AUTUMN *reaping the harvest*

But most of all I shall remember the Monarchs,
that unhurried westward drift of one small winged form after
another, each drawn by some invisible force. We talked a little
about their migration, their life history. Did they return?
We thought not; for most, at least, this was the closing journey
of their lives. . . . we had felt no sadness when we spoke
of the fact that there would be no return. And rightly—for when
any living thing comes to the end of its life cycle we accept
that end as natural.

— Rachael Carson,
Lost Woods

I am like a vine putting out graceful shoots,
My blossoms bear the fruit of glory and wealth.
Approach me, you who desire me,
And take your fill of my fruits.

— Wisdom, in Sirach 24:17–19

My heart is moved by all I cannot save;
so much has been destroyed. I have cast my lot with those
who age after age, perversely, with no extraordinary power,
reconstitute the world.

— Adrienne Rich,
The Dream of a Common Language,
Poems 1974–1977

Autumn is a season of changes. In many parts of the world it brings with it a shower of earth colors. The spirits of fulfillment and abundance, transition and transformation replenish the Earth. This is the harvest season, universally a time for rejoicing and giving thanks. We see trees changing colors, smell ripe apples and cider, taste the fruits of the harvest, hear leaves crunch under foot, touch pumpkins, and feel the crisp air.

This season opens us to changes and shifting patterns in our lives. It calls us to share abundance and make room for the new. It reminds us to store up some of the harvest extras for the winter when we will need nourishment. This season of transition calls us to notice change we may want to make to be healthier and to help the Earth survive.

The ecofeminist liturgies in this section focus the themes of ripeness, fullness, transitions, change, abundance, harvest. They use symbols such as leaves, harvest fruits and vegetables, corn, apples, grapes, corn bread, cider, compost. They urge us to heal the Earth in autumn by making a compost bin, composting kitchen scraps and leaves, planting spring bulbs. Use them as models to celebrate the autumn festivals of September 21 (March 21), autumn equinox; Sukkot; October 31, Halloween; November 1, All Saints Day; November 2, All Souls Day; third Thursday of November (in the United States), Thanksgiving.

eleven

DEEP PEACE OF THE CHANGING SEASONS TO YOU

Generations before us have been attentive to the changes in autumn. The autumn equinox, on about September 21 (March 21), balances the dark and the light, life and death, sleep and wakefulness. Once again night and day are of equal length: twelve hours each. Autumn is beginning. Daylight is decreasing. Festivals of this changing season invite us to look at the transitions within ourselves, our spirituality, our relationships, and our society. Change is a part of living, as the seasons teach us yearly.

This liturgy focuses on spiritual change, inviting participants to describe connections to their religious past and spiritual future and to give thanks for the insights they have received. To close, they connect with the deep peace of the running waves, the flowing air, the quiet Earth, and the shining stars. It is powerful during harvest or transition times.

Preparation

In the center of a circle of chairs, one for each participant, place three candles, corn bread, wheat bread, cider, and wine on a harvest cloth. Involve as many people as possible in leading various parts of this liturgy.

Naming the Circle

To begin, let us give one another a glimpse of who we are by saying our names and speaking a word about changes we notice at this season, changes or transitions inside of us or around us. (*Naming*)

Call to Gather

Autumn is a season of change. The shifting patterns are imperceptible to some, and obvious to others. Tonight we will reflect together on our changes, what we inevitably give up to make room for the new, what we store up for the winter when we will need something extra. We often tend to think we can just add on or pile up, but the fact is that we have to let go in order to make room. We trim the branches, plow under the vegetation that will renew the soil for next year. We stock shelves of the pantry at this season in order to use fruits of the harvest for the winter. We store up in order to use what we need. So the paradox—harvesting only to use.

Our interest in this autumn season of transition is to look at our spirituality, what grounds us as we move through the cycle. For many of us, the "faith of our fathers" is not the faith of our future, nor is the faith of our great-grandmothers really ours either: patriarchal Christianity and romanticized matriarchies do not fully satisfy us. But what replaces all of this? What is the real content of calling ourselves women-church, discipleship of equals, a spiritual community of struggle? Are there certain things we can say and do together that give spiritual shape to the movement and spiritual grounding to our lives?

This liturgy is not an effort to write a common creed, but it is a time to assess and reassess what we believe individually and as a group. This is a time and a place to be safe, to explore, to be confident that regardless of our changes the divine love that holds us all will prevail.

Let us center ourselves to celebrate "Deep Peace of the Changing Seasons to You," a liturgy of three movements.

FIRST MOVEMENT

Song: "Sing a Gentle Love Song," by Kathy Sherman

> Sing a gentle love song to the earth,
> Fill the air with music for her healing.
> Then be still and you will hear
> Her love song forever sung to you.[1]

Reading: "The Spiritual, Political Journey," by Emily Culpepper

(The reader lights a candle.)

We were discussing the issue of connection to one's religious past. Knowing I no longer identified as Christian, one of the women asked, "But you do draw on it in some ways still, don't you? Would you speak of it as your roots?" I paused, searching for words. That phrase has never felt quite right to me. From the root springs the tree; they are a continuous growth. The ecology of my spiritual life is more complex than that, with moments of radical discontinuity and continuity. "Compost," I heard myself say. And again, with an increasing sense of satisfaction that at last I had found the apt metaphor, "Compost. My Christianity has become compost." It has decayed and died, becoming a mix of animate and inanimate, stinking rot and released nutrients. Humus. Fertilizer. The part of organic life cycles with which everyone gets uncomfortable and skips over in the rush to rhapsodize growth and progress and blossoms and fruition and rebirth. But in between is the dark, rich mysterious stage, when life decomposes into soil. It is a sacred time—like the dark no moon new moon in my meditations, that liminal stage and dangerous essential passage between the last slender waning crescent and the first shred of a shining waxing new one. Compost. A pile of organic substance transforming into a ground, a matrix into which we must mix other elements for the next seeds to sprout. Other vital forces must wet and warm the matrix. And additional deaths, so inevitable in changing/living, will need to feed this ground. Humus. It is from this that we are named, human, to acknowledge our connection to the earth, the place where we stand in the vast living universe. If our traditions and symbols are truly part of living, then they are organic and will have rhythms of living and dying.[2]

Reflection

How do you describe your connection to your religious past, to your spiritual future? Think for a moment, then turn to someone next to you and share your reflection. (*Sharing*)

SECOND MOVEMENT

Song: "Sing a Gentle Love Song"

> Sing a gentle love song to the earth,
> Fill the air with music for her healing.
> Then be still and you will hear
> Her love song forever sung to you.

Telling the Story

(*The reader lights a candle.*)

Demeter is the Greek goddess of agriculture, the giver of crops; her daughter Kore, or Persephone, is the grain-maiden, the symbol of new growth. Each year after the harvest Demeter lets go of her daughter, who goes beneath the Earth to rule the underworld. Demeter grieves at the separation, wanders the land searching for her daughter, and declares that nothing will grow until Kore returns. And each spring, when Kore comes back, abundance and fertility return to the Earth.

Reflection

What are you letting go of or releasing? What are you grieving separation from? Think for a moment, then turn to another person and share your reflections. (*Sharing*)

THIRD MOVEMENT

Song: "Sing a Gentle Love Song"

> Sing a gentle love song to the earth,
> Fill the air with music for her healing.
> Then be still and you will hear
> Her love song forever sung to you.

Reading: "Mother Corn," by Polingaysi Qoyawayma (Hopi teacher)
(*The reader lights a candle.*)

Mother Corn has fed you as she has fed all Hopi people, since the long, long ago when she was no longer than my thumb. Mother Corn is the promise of food and life. I grind with gratitude for the richness of our harvest, not with cross feelings of working too hard. As I kneel at my grinding stone, I bow my head in prayer, thanking the great forces for provision. I have received much. I am willing to give much in return, for as I have taught you, there must always be a giving back for what one receives.[3]

Reflection

What have you received spiritually for which you are grateful? Think for a moment and share with everyone. (*Sharing*)

The changing season calls us to stand in a circle, put our arms around one another, create our community to acknowledge that we are coming home to ourselves and one another as we change.

Song: "Coming Home," by Carolyn McDade

> We're coming home to the spirit in our soul.
> We're coming home
> And the healing makes us whole.
> Like rivers running to the sea
> We're coming home, we're coming home.
>
> As the day is woven into night,
> As the darkness lives within the light,
> As we open vision to new sight,
> We're coming home, we're coming home.[4]

Blessing and Sharing the Breads and Drinks

(Invite one person to bless corn bread and wheat bread, and another to bless cider and wine. These blessings will be spontaneous and flow from the movements of the liturgy.)

Sending Forth

Echo me when I gesture to you with my hand. *(The leader gestures for participants to echo the first and last line of each stanza.)*

> Peace of the flowing stream be yours, *(Echo)*
> Water flowing, cleansing and healing.
> May you be refreshed.
> Peace of the flowing stream be yours. *(Echo)*
>
> Peace of the gentle breeze be yours, *(Echo)*
> Winds blowing, stirring, cooling,
> May you breathe deeply.
> Peace of the gentle breeze be yours. *(Echo)*
>
> Peace of the fertile earth be yours, *(Echo)*
> Land giving life to diverse creatures.
> May you walk on firm ground.
> Peace of the fertile earth be yours. *(Echo)*

Peace of the twinkling stars be yours, *(Echo)*
Lights shining, sparkling, beaming,
May your journey be filled with wonder.
Peace of the twinkling stars be yours. *(Echo)*

Add your own wish for peace.

Greeting of Peace

Filled with this deep peace, let us bless one another with embraces of peace. *(Blessing)*

Song: "Coming Home," by Carolyn McDade

We're coming home to the spirit in our soul.
We're coming home and the healing makes us whole.
Like rivers running to the sea,
We're coming home, we're coming home.

To reclaim the thinking of our minds,
Leaving shackles lying far behind,
Bearing hope for every soul confined,
We're coming home, we're coming home.

NOTES

1. "Sing a Gentle Love Song" by Kathy Sherman, CSJ, from *Gather the Dreamers* © 1991. Courtesy of the Ministry of the Arts, Sisters of St. Joseph, LaGrange, IL. www.ministryofthearts.org. Audio recording.

2. In Paula Cooey, William. R. Eakin, and Jay. B. McDaniel, eds., *After Patriarchy: Feminist Transformations of the World Religions* (Maryknoll, NY: Orbis Books, 1991), 162–63.

3. In Polingaysi Qoyawayma, *No Turning Back*. As told to Vada F. Carlson (Albuquerque: University of New Mexico Press, 1964), 71.

4. From McDade, *This Ancient Love*. © 1990, Surtsey Publishing. Audio recording.

twelve

A WOMEN'S HARVEST FESTIVAL

This autumn festival celebrates a harvest that is often overlooked: the contributions of women. The ceremony welcomes guests into a harvest shelter to remember women's stories.

This liturgy honors the ancestors who have passed on to us over the generations their wisdom and insights, their memories of the past and present. It honors women who have gone before us and made the world a more livable place for us and for the next generations. Participants are invited to intertwine their stories with those of biblical women, church mothers, goddesses, women of recorded history, the lost generations, grandmothers, and mothers.

Preparation

Build (outdoors) a rectangular booth that has four enclosed sides and a roof that is open to the stars. Use twelve pieces of lumber, each 1" x 2" x 8', for the frame and brace the corners. Using a staple gun, attach decorative cloths to the four sides, leaving a flap open for an entrance. Lightly weave branches and corn stalks across the top for a partial roof.

Place four candles, a loaf of hallah, apples and honey, fruit, matzoh, and cold tea, enough for your group, on an altar inside the dwelling. This ceremony is a simple meal that lasts for a few hours, so prepare the participants.

Call to Gather

Welcome to our Women's Harvest Festival. Tonight we duplicate the wandering in the desert of our mothers as we sit in a shelter built open to the sky. This ceremony, which is related to the Latin word *hospes*, or guest, is based on one developed in the Jewish mystical traditions of the Middle Ages. In it, ancestors were welcomed into the booth, called a sukkah, built during the Holiday of Shelter. In our festival here tonight, we welcome you, all of our ancestors, and women's memories of the past and present to share this time and space with us now. We invite you to share your symbols, your memories, and your stories with us. By recollecting the past, we strengthen the present and enhance the future.

Our liturgy is divided into four sections. The first focuses upon our mythical and ancient ancestors: biblical women, church mothers, goddesses from the past, and women from other traditions of long ago. The second is closer historically but culturally broader: we include here the "herstories" of South American women, Asian women, Native American women, and others. The third section recalls a lost generation: the women and children of the Holocaust. Our fourth returns us to ourselves, and we recall our own lives, families, and stories. After each section, there will be time for each of us to share a memory and thus add our links to the chain of recorded women's history.

The four candles on the table symbolize the four parts of this ceremony. We invite women from the north, south, east, and west to join us in our harvest festival.

Naming the Circle

We begin by introducing ourselves and breaking bread together. As we go around the circle, speak your name and take a piece of bread that we will bless and eat together when the naming is completed. (*Naming*)

Blessing the Bread

(*When all have bread, someone lifts the bread, saying:*) Please pray after me:

> Blessed are you, Source of Creation,
> Who brings forth bread from the Earth. (*Echo*)

Song: "L'chi Lach," by Debbie Friedman

(*In Genesis God said to Sarah and Abraham, "Get yourself out to a land that I will show you." L'chi lach is Hebrew, feminine form, for "Get yourself out." L'chi lecha is masculine form. The final phrase, "l'simchat chayim" means "toward the joy or rejoicing of life."*)

> L'chi lach, to a land that I will show you.
> L'chi lecha, to a place you do not know.
> L'chi lach, on your journey I will bless you.
> And you shall be a blessing,
> You shall be a blessing,
> You shall be a blessing, l'chi lach.
>
> L'chi lach, and I shall make your name great.
> L'chi lecha, and all shall praise your name.
> L'chi lach, to the place that I will show you.
> And you shall be a blessing,

You shall be a blessing,
You shall be a blessing, l'chi lach.

L'simchat chayim, l'simchat chayim, l'simchat chayim,
l'chi lach.[1]

FIRST MOVEMENT: BIBLICAL WOMEN, CHURCH MOTHERS, GODDESSES

Lighting the Candle

(Someone lights a candle, lifts it, and says:) We invite the women of our earliest recorded traditions to join us in our harvest festival—biblical women, church mothers, and goddesses.

Sharing the Apples and Honey

We begin by sharing apple and honey together; by this, we reclaim the apple as a positive symbol of women's history. The honey symbolizes our hopes that our present recollections of the past will help sweeten the future by renewing our commitment to ourselves. Take a piece of apple and dip it in the honey. *(Pass a bowl of apple slices and honey around the circle.)*

Blessing the Daughters

We recite the traditional blessing said by Jewish parents over their daughters. Please repeat after me:

> May God make you like Sarah, Hagar, Rebecca, Leah, and Rachel. *(Echo)*

Welcome, Biblical Women: "Song of Praise," by Elisabeth Schüssler Fiorenza

> A wandering Aramean was my mother.
> In Egypt she bore slaves.
> Then she called to the God of our mothers

Sarah, Hagar, Rebecca, Rachel, Leah.
Praise God Who Hears, Forever.

A warrior, judge, and harlot was my mother
God called her from time to time
to save and liberate her people
Miriam, Jael, Deborah, Judith, Tamar
Praise God Who Saves, Forever.

A Galilean Jew was my mother.
She bore a wonderful child
to be persecuted, hated and executed.
Mary, mother of sorrows, mother of us all.
Praise God Who Gives Strength, Forever.

A witness to Christ's resurrection was my mother.
The apostle to the apostles
Rejected, forgotten, proclaimed a whore
Mary of Magdala, foundation of women-church
Praise God Who Lives, Forever.

An apostle, prophet, founder, and teacher was my mother
called to the discipleship of equals
Empowered by the Sophia-God of Jesus
Junia, Priscilla, Myrta, Nympha, Thecla
Praise God Who Calls, Forever.

A faithful Christian woman was my mother,
A mystic, witch, martyr, heretic, saint, uppity woman
A black slave, a poor imigrant, an old hag, a wise woman
    was my mother
May we, with her, in every generation
Praise God Who Images Us All.[2]

Welcome, the Goddess: "The Goddess," by Starhawk

The Goddess is the first of all earth, the dark, nurturing mother who brings forth all life. She is the power of fertility and generation; the womb, and also the receptive tomb, the power of death. All proceeds from Her; all returns to Her. As earth, She is also plant life; trees, the herbs and grains that sustain life. She is the body, and the body is sacred.[3]

Sharing A Memory

You who have a memory related to these ancient traditions, share your story with us now. (*Sharing*)

Song: "You Can't Kill the Spirit," traditional

> You can't kill the spirit, She's like a mountain
> Old and strong, she lives on and on and on.[4]

SECOND MOVEMENT: WOMEN OF RECORDED HISTORY

Lighting the Candle

(*Someone lights the second candle and says:*) We invite women out of our recorded history, women from our own and other cultures, to intertwine their stories with ours during our harvest feast. We begin this section by sharing fruits that, while harvested in the United States, are indigenous to other parts of the world.

Blessing the Source

Please say after me: Praised is the source of the multitudes of fruit on the Earth. (*Echo*)

Welcome, Sojourner Truth: "Ar'n't I a Woman?"
by Sojourner Truth

Look at my arm! [And she bared her right arm to the shoulder, showing her tremendous muscular power.] I have ploughed, and planted, and gathered into barns, and no man could head me—

and ar'n't I a woman? I could work as much and eat as much as a man (when I could get it) and bear the lash as well—and ar'n't I a woman? I have borne thirteen chilern, and seen 'em mos' sold into slavery, and when I cried out with my mother's grief, none but Jesus heard me—and ar'n't I a woman?[5]

Welcome, Mothers of the Disappeared: "When Jorge Disappeared," by Hebe de Bonafini

The Mothers and Grandmothers of the Plaza de Mayo in Argentina and the Co-Madres in El Salvador wear white hand-kerchiefs on their heads to symbolize their search for their disap-peared loved ones.

When Jorge disappeared my first reaction was to rush out des-perately to look for him. I didn't cry. I didn't tear out my hair. Nothing mattered any more except that I should find him, that I should go everywhere, at any time, day or night. I didn't want to read anything about what was happening, just search, search. Then I realized we had to look for all of them and that we had to be together because together we were stronger. We had no previ-ous political experience. We had no contacts. We knew no one. We made mistakes at first, but we learnt quickly. Every door slammed in our faces made us stop and think, made us stronger. We learnt quickly and we never gave up. Everything they said we shouldn't do, that we weren't able to do, we proved we could do.[6]

Welcome, Indigenous Women: Excerpt from "Word and Language: a Haggle," by Paula Gunn Allen

There is an enormous difference between the way western people approach the use of language and the way tribal people approach it. [Tribal people] say the words are sacred. We don't mean that you are supposed to kneel down and worship them. We mean that you should in your being recognize that when you speak, your utterance has consequences inwardly and outwardly and that you are accountable for those consequences. You can't just say anything that comes to your head and then get distressed if another person acts on it. Now that other person many have misunderstood you, which means that they have a responsibility to find out exactly what you mean before they act, but the principle. It is still there. Without linguistic honor there can be no community, there can be no ethic, there can be no love, there can be no creative vision, there can be no peace, and there can be no relationship.[7]

Welcome *Han*-ridden Spirits: "I Come from the Land of the Spirits," by Chung Hyun-Kyung

I come from Korea, the land of spirits full of *Han. Han* is anger. *Han* is resentment. *Han* is bitterness. *Han* is grief. *Han* is brokenheartedness and the raw energy for the struggle for liberation. In my tradition, people who were killed or died unjustly became wandering spirits, the *Han*-ridden spirits. They are all over the place seeking the chance to make the wrong right. Therefore the living people's responsibility is to listen to the voices of the *Han*-ridden spirits and to participate in the spirits' work of making right whatever is wrong.

These *Han*-ridden spirits in our people's history have been agents through whom the Holy Spirit has spoken her compassion and wisdom for life. Without hearing the cries of these spirits, we cannot hear the voice of the Holy Spirit. . . . They are the icons of the Holy Spirit who became tangible and visible to us. Because of them we can feel, touch and taste the concrete bodily historical presence of the Holy Spirit in our midst . . .[8]

Sharing A Memory

You who have a story or a memory to share about women from recorded history, tell us now. (*Sharing*)

Song

> You can't kill the spirit, she's like a mountain
> Old and strong, she lives on and on and on.

THIRD MOVEMENT: THE LOST GENERATION

Lighting the Candle

(*Someone lights a candle, lifts it, and says:*) We invite the women and children of the Holocaust to find shelter in our sukkah. This generation was lost. To the Nazis, women and children had little labor value, so most were killed immediately upon reaching the death camps. It is for us to tell their stories so that their memory is not lost. We begin this section by sharing matzoh, the bread of affliction, and cold weak tea. There was no abundance of food for this generation.

Blessing the Souls

Please say after me: Praised are the souls of the living and the dead. (*Echo*)

Welcome, Young Women: From 15 July 1944, by Anne Frank

It's really a wonder that I haven't dropped all my ideals, because they seem so absurd and impossible to carry out. Yet I keep them, because in spite of everything I still believe that people are really good at heart. I simply can't build up my hopes on a foundation consisting of confusion, misery, and death.

I can see the world gradually being turned into a wilderness. I hear the ever-approaching thunder, which will destroy us too. I can feel the sufferings of millions—and yet, if I look into the heavens, I think that it will all come out right, that this cruelty too will end, and that peace and tranquility will return again.

In the meantime, I must uphold my ideals, for perhaps the time will come when I shall be able to carry them out.[9]

Welcome, Women Liaisons: From Belgium, "From Death to Hope: A Catholic/Jewish Service," by Eugene Fisher and Leon Klenicki

In May 1943, Mme. Marthe De Smet of Dilbeek, in the countryside near Brussels, received a telephone call from Sr. Claire, a nun at the Convent des Soeurs de Tres St. Sauveur in the city. Was she willing to hide another Jewish child, the caller asked.

The situation was desperate. The nuns had hidden fifteen little Jewish girls until their hiding place was betrayed to the Gestapo. Just hours before the Gestapo's truck arrived to take the children to their death, the nuns had somehow gotten word to the underground. The children had been hastily moved under cover of darkness and then placed in safe but temporary homes. Now, it was essential to find a permanent hiding place for each of them.

Sr. Claire knew that the De Smets—Georges, his wife, Marthe, and their children, Marie-Paule, Andre, Eliane, and Francis—were already hiding a Jewish child, three-year-old Regine Monk. Nonetheless, she was confident that Mme. De Smet would not turn her down. She was right. A few days later, three-year-old Yvette Lerner came into the De Smet household, to be safely sheltered there until the liberation of Brussels in September 1944. Shortly after her arrival, the De Smets took a third child, then an infant, Liliane Klein.

At risk of their own lives and those of their children, the De Smets embarked on a course of active opposition to the Nazis' plan for the extermination of all Jews. In this, they were motivated by deep religious conviction and by a strong love of children.

After the war, the De Smets refused all remuneration and asked only for the continued friendship of the families to whom they had given so much.[10]

Welcome, the Dead and the Survivors: "Each of Us Has a Name," by Zelda

Each of us has a name
Given by the source of life
And given by our parents.
Each of us has a name
Given by our stature and our smile
And given by what we wear.

Each of us has a name
Given by the mountains
And given by our walls.

Each of us has a name
Given by the stars
And given by our neighbors.

Each of us has a name
Given by our sins
And given by our longing.

Each of us has a name
Given by our enemies
And given by our love.

Each of us has a name
Given by our celebrations
And given by our work.

Each of us has a name
Given by the seasons
And given by our blindness.

Each of us has a name
Given by the sea
And given by
Our death.[11]

Sharing A Memory

Share with us a story or a question about the lost generations now. (*Sharing*)

Song

> You can't kill the spirit, she's like a mountain
> Old and strong, she lives on and on and on.

FOURTH MOVEMENT: PERSONAL STORIES

Lighting the Candle

(*Someone lights the fourth candle and says:*) Our fourth section contains our own personal stories. We tell the stories of the women who have accompanied us on our journeys: who, with steadying hand, soothing word, or courageous example, have helped us to get honey from rock and water from stone. To begin this section, we again break bread together, completing our circular journey.

Blessing the Women

Please say after me: Praised are the mothers, sisters, and daughters who have ever kneaded bread. (*Echo*)

Welcome, Grandmothers: "To Anowa," by Mercy Oduyoye

(dedicated to Armah and Aidoo)

> Anowa, the mythic woman ancestor from whom my race
> takes its origin
> Anowa, glowing by the light of the communal fire which
> you lit, you who hold the secret of fire. The Black and
> Beautiful One, Image and Glory of the Nation
> Anowa, woman, attending more to peace than to the
> glamour of heroic deeds, shunning the institutions of
> monarchy, absolute power and exclusive authority.
> Anowa, who says to them what they do to you: Mother, they
> are doing us evil.

Mother, you learnt to hunt but not for fun.
The aged lion who in his impotence turns to tyrannic
humans.
The wild dog who delights in rooting out more than
he can eat.
The cowardly hyena sneaking around to pound on the
weak and the infirm.
These, the enemies of Anowa's children are Anowa's prey.
Anowa may your arm be strong against our foes.
Anowa, the Black woman who pursues the self-seeking
white death and male-tombstones. To you and all who
claim you as mother, tombstones mean nothing![12]

Welcome, Mothers: Excerpt from *In Search of Our Mothers' Gardens*, by Alice Walker

My mother adorned with flowers whatever shabby house we were forced to live in. And not just your typical straggly country strand of zinnias, either. She planted ambitious gardens—and still does—with over fifty different varieties of plants that bloom profusely from early March until late November. . . .

Whatever she planted grew as if by magic, and her fame as a grower of flowers spread over three counties. Because of her creativity with her flowers, even my memories of poverty are seen through a screen of blossoms—sunflowers, petunias, roses, dahlias, forsythia, spirea, delphiniums, verbena . . . and on and on.

And I remember people coming to my mother's yard to be given cuttings from her flowers; I heard again the praise showered on her because whatever rocky soil she landed on, she turned into a garden. A garden so brilliant with colors, so original in its design, so magnificent with life and creativity, that to this day people drive by our house in Georgia—perfect strangers and imperfect strangers—and ask to stand or walk among my mother's art.[13]

Welcome, Ourselves: "I Come from the Earth," by Marie Ropeti

> I come from the Earth,
> I am a child of the Earth,
> the source of life
> where my placenta is buried.
> My connection is made
> source of my life.[14]

Sharing A Memory

If you wish, share a piece of your story. *(Sharing)*

Song

> You can't kill the spirit, she's like a mountain
> Old and strong, she lives on and on and on.

Sending Forth

Together with all the souls we have gathered into our sukkah tonight, we remember that we are all guests. We recall our matriarchs, we celebrate women from all cultures, we commemorate the women of the Holocaust, and we appreciate ourselves. By claiming what is ours from the past, we enable our daughters to create the future. This year we are still enslaved; next year we may be free!

Song and Spiral Dance: "Dancing Sophia's Circle," by Colleen Fulmer

> Ring us round, O ancient circle,
> Great Mother dancing free,
> Beauty, strength, and Holy Wisdom,
> Blessing you and blessing me.[15]

NOTES

1. "L'chi Lach," by Debbie Friedman and Savino Teubal (based on Genesis 12:1–2), *And You Shall Be a Blessing* © 1988, Sounds Write Productions, Inc. Audio recording.

2. Revised by Elisabeth Schüssler Fiorenza from Mother Thunder Mission, "A Wandering Aramean Was My Mother," in *No Longer Strangers* (Geneva, Switzerland: WCC Publications, 1983), 41. Also in *Worcester Connection*, vol. 1, issue 1 (Center for Reflective Action, 21 Crown Street, Worcester, MA 01609).

3. Starhawk, *The Spiral Dance: A Rebirth of the Ancient Religion of the Dark Goddess* (San Francisco: HarperCollins, 1979), 78.

4. "You Can't Kill the Spirit," traditional.

5. Sojourner Truth (1851), "Ar'n't I A Woman?" in Olive Gilbert, *Narrative of Sojourner Truth: A Bondswoman of Olden Time, with a History of Her* (New York: Penguin Books, 1998), 92.

6. In Jo Fisher, *Mothers of the Disappeared* (Boston: South End Press, 1989), 52.

7. Originally appeared in *Mama Bear's News and Notes* (20 July 1986).

8. In Lynda Katsuno-Ishii and Edna J. Orteza, eds. *Of Rolling Waters and Roaring Wind: A Celebration of the Woman Song* (Geneva, Switzerland: WCC Publications, 2000), 6.

9. Anne Frank, *The Diary of Anne Frank*, 15 July 1944.

10. From Belgium, in *Liturgies on the Holocaust*, ed., Marcia Sachs Littell and Sharon Weissman Gutman (Valley Forge, PA: Trinity Press International, 1996), 39.

11. Translated by Marcia Falk in Falk's *The Book of Blessings: New Jewish Prayers for Daily Life, the Sabbath, and the New Moon Festival* (San Francisco: HarperCollins, 1996), 106–9.

12. In Anna Karin Hammar and Anne-Marie Kappeli, eds., *Prayers and Poems, Songs and Stories* (Geneva, Switzerland, WCC Publications, 1988), 40.

13. Walker, *In Search of Our Mothers' Gardens*, 241.

14. In Lynda Katsuno-Ishii and Edna J. Orteza, eds., *Of Rolling Waters and Roaring Wind* (Geneva, Switzerland: WCC Publications, 2000), 6.

15. From Fulmer, *Dancing Sophia's Circle*.

thirteen

THE ROARING OF CREATION AS CRIES FOR ECOJUSTICE

The Earth is crying for protection. Creation is roaring for safety. From generation to generation our planet's inhabitants need a safe place that will be home for all our relations. We must restore the Earth to dignity.

This liturgy invites participants to hear creation's cries for ecojustice, and to take action to restore the Earth to its dignity. They begin by walking and listening to the Earth. Hearing cries for ecojustice, they declare, "We must work for ecojustice." They reflect on how their lifestyles affect the survival of planet Earth.

Preparation

You will need a globe of the world and symbols for each of the four elements—air (incense, chimes, or gesture to the wind), fire (a candle or bonfire), water (a bowl of water), earth (a pot of soil, compost, or touch the ground).

Call to Gather

(Invite people to sit on the ground in a circle or, if it is raining, stand on a covered porch and listen to the rain.)

In the name of the Creator who gave birth to all—trees, lakes, flowers, animals, and humans—welcome to our liturgy, "The Roaring of Creation as Cries for Ecojustice." This Earth is a sacred space, the source of all life. We are all made of the planet's elemental energies—air, fire, water, and earth. That is what I am. That is what you are. That is what all creation is.

We are called by our Loving Creator to treasure these elements and all life, to protect them from abuse. All creation cries out for our respect and care.

Today we declare a retreat, a time of reflection to listen to the cries for ecojustice and to commit ourselves to restore the Earth to its dignity. Let us walk in silence and listen to the Earth. *(Walking)*

Hymn: "Designer, Creator, Most Provident God," by Jane Parker Huber

Designer, Creator, most provident God,
We praise you for forests and mountains and sod,
For life-giving water in river and lake,
For life more abundant for all the world's sake.

We pray that your people will find in this place
Full measures, o'er flowing, of love and of grace,
Of challenging thought and of nurturing care
Of deepening friendships and strengthening prayer.

The music of silence caressing your ears
Renews us in spirit and eases our fears.
We listen, we ponder, we wait for your voice,
And hearing, in gratitude, now we rejoice.[1]

Naming the Circle

Today, as we reconnect with the Earth, let us take time to create our community. Take the globe, speak your name, say "I will restore the Earth to its dignity," and pass the globe to the person on your left. (*When the globe returns to the person who first passed it, that person puts it in the center of the circle.*)

Prayer of Confession

Praise be to You, Creator of All Things Living,
Today we confess that we have forgotten our interconnection with your universe.
We confess that we have alienated ourselves from the cosmos.
We confess that we have been indifferent to the environmental crises that loom large on the horizon of our survival.
We confess that we, our sisters, brothers, and children, have abused your creation through ignorance, exploitation, and greed.
We confess doing permanent damage to your handiwork.
We confess to alienating ourselves from the Source of All Life.
We confess that we have forgotten who we are.
We confess . . . (*Please add your own.*)
Forgiving Creator, awaken us to the roaring of creation, the cries for ecojustice, that we may open our minds and hearts to respond.

Litany for Ecojustice

(*Two people read alternately.*)
Please respond to each cry for ecojustice with the words, "We must work for ecojustice."

LEADER ONE: Because many refuse to acknowledge that the Earth is a living, interrelated system,

RESPONSE: **We must work for ecojustice.**

LEADER TWO: Because too many people have degraded fertile Earth into landfills, forests into deserts, running rivers into silted floodplains,

RESPONSE: **We must work for ecojustice.**

LEADER ONE: Because grave assaults on the biosphere—acid rain, desertification, waste accumulation, overpopulation, ozone depletion—rob us all of our heritage,

RESPONSE: **We must work for ecojustice.**

LEADER TWO: Because governments and corporations play economic and environmental concerns off against each other,

RESPONSE: **We must work for ecojustice.**

LEADER ONE: Because industrial countries persist in lifestyles, policies, and production methods that endanger human existence and exploit the rest of the world,

RESPONSE: **We must work for ecojustice.**

LEADER TWO: Because many use power to dominate humans and nature,

RESPONSE: **We must work for ecojustice.**

LEADER ONE: Because materialism leaves a spiritual vacuum, a pervasive alienation where people have grown isolated from nature and from each other,

RESPONSE: **We must work for ecojustice.**

LEADER TWO: Because we have forgotten our rootedness in an integrated way of life,

RESPONSE: **We must work for ecojustice.**

LEADER ONE: Because vast natural areas have been rendered unfit for habitation by plants and animals and are now becoming unfit for human habitation as well,

RESPONSE: **We must work for ecojustice.**

LEADER TWO: Because some species are endangered and even extinct as a result of destroyed habitats,

RESPONSE: **We must work for ecojustice.**

LEADER ONE: Because many commercial products are tested on animals in painful ways,

RESPONSE: **We must work for ecojustice.**

LEADER TWO: Because deforestation displaces indigenous peoples; hazardous waste sites are located near poor neighborhoods; industrialized factory farms eliminate the small family farmer; and international policies of free trade hurt the Earth and its inhabitants,

RESPONSE: **We must work for ecojustice.**

LEADERS ONE AND TWO: Because each form of life is integrated with every other form of life, and because we have not rallied to the Earth's defense,

RESPONSE: **We must work for ecojustice.**

Hymn: "Let Us Feel the Breeze Together," tune "Let Us Break Bread Together"

> Let us feel the breeze together, we are one (*Repeat*)
> When we kill forests and farms with our exploitation,
> O God, have mercy on us.

> Let us build fires together, we are one (*Repeat*)
> When we burn land and oil with our exploitation,
> O God, have mercy on us.

Let us touch the Earth gently, we are one (*Repeat*)
When we scar planet Earth with our exploitation,
O God, have mercy on us.

Let us drink water together, we are one (*Repeat*)
When we pollute rivers and seas with our exploitation,
O God, have mercy on us.[2]

Reflection

Let us reflect silently on the cries for ecojustice that we have heard. (*Pause*) How will I respond? What action will I take to restore the Earth to its dignity and help the planet survive? How do my daily habits affect the survival of life on planet Earth? How can I change my lifestyle so that it reflects and enables a sustainable future for all of us and all our relations? (*Pause*)

Invite a word of commitment to emerge from within you. (*Pause*) Touch one of the elements—air, fire, water, earth—and speak aloud your word of commitment. (*Sharing*)

Hymn: "Designer, Creator, Most Provident God," by Jane Parker Huber

You call us to justice, to freedom and peace,
To work building bridges that love may increase.
Stand with us to show us the excellent way
To welcome, unhindered, your long-promised day.[3]

Prayer of Gratitude

Let us pray together. Follow my movements.
May it be beautiful before me. (*Hands stretched out in front.*)
May it be beautiful behind me. (*Hands stretched out behind.*)
May it be beautiful below me. (*Hands stretched down to feet.*)
May it be beautiful above me. (*Hands raised toward sky.*)
May it be beautiful all around me. (*Turn around,
    with outstretched arms.*)
In beauty it is finished. (*Arch arms above head.*)

Sending Forth

Filled with the roaring of creation,
    let us go forth restless and disturbed
    by the senseless exploitation and destruction of the Earth.
Filled with the beauty of creation and strengthened
      by our commitments,
    let us go forth to restore the Earth to its dignity.

The blessing of the God of Sarah and of Abraham,
The blessing of Jesus, born of the woman Mary,
The blessing of the Holy Spirit who protects us as a mother
    with her children,
Be with all our relations.
Amen. Blessed be. Let it be so.

NOTES

1. From *A Singing Faith* by Jane Parker Huber, 12. © 1987 Jane Parker Huber. Used by permission of Westminster John Knox Press.

2. Adapted by Diann Neu.

3. Huber, *A Singing Faith*, 12.

fourteen

HALLOWED BE THE
TURNING INTO DARKNESS

As the Wheel of the Year turns, light declines and darkness increases in the northern hemisphere. Festivals at this time invite us to think about our own mortality. October 31 is Halloween, Samhain, the season of the dead. November 1 celebrates the Feast of the Dead in Mexico and All Saints Day in the Christian calendar. November 2 memorializes All Souls Day. This trilogy of feasts honors the ancestors who have gone before us and still live among us.

This liturgy celebrates the closeness of the worlds of the living and dead. Use it for any of the above named feasts or to celebrate the trilogy of the season. It invites participants to remember the dead, take a look at death, and focus on what is ending, dying, or needs to die in their own lives.

Preparation

Arrange a loaf of bread in a basket with sliced fruits and nuts. Place this basket on a central table, along with a glass of cider, black and white candles, an incensor or smudge stick, a crystal, and a bowl.

Call to Gather

This is the time of year for the annual meeting of the many worlds, when past and future are at ease with the present, when those of us with bodies get together with the spirits of those who preceded us. We come to the crossroads between the season of life and the season of death. Halloween, October 31; All Saints Day, November 1; and All Souls Day, November 2, are times to remember our ancestors.

During these nights the veil between life and death is thin; the two worlds come close together. There is much movement back and forth through the veil that makes it possible to get in touch with the spirits on either side. Tonight we hallow this turning into darkness and spend time with those who have died. We remember our own mortality.

Naming the Circle

Let us hallow this space by saying our names and incensing one another. Smudging or incensing is a ritual burning of herbs, using the smoke produced to purify a space and the people in it. Ascending smoke symbolically forms a channel connecting us to Great Spirits, Holy Ones who have gone before us, the Communion of Saints.

Let us pass the incensor or smudge stick from person to person and purify one another. Hold the smoking herbs in your nondominant hand, stay a few feet away from the person, and use gentle, short movements with your dominant hand to direct the smoke toward the person. Go down the front of the body, from head to feet, with the smoke. Then repeat the procedure down the back, from head to feet.

Those receiving the incense cup their hands and bring the smoke in toward their bodies. *(Smudging)*

Song: "Sisters' Spiral," by Colleen Fulmer

(This is a two-part circular canon.)

> Spiraling, spiraling circle of Wisdom
> Sisters together a body of praise.
>
> Born of Earth her rhythms, cycles
> Love that's flowing from ancient of days.[1]

Reading: "All Souls," by May Sarton

> Did someone say that there would be an end,
> An end, Oh, an end, to love and mourning?
> Such voices speak when sleep and waking blend,
> The cold bleak voices of the early morning
> When all the birds are dumb in dark November—
> Remember and forget, forget, remember.
>
> After the false night, warm true voices, wake!
> Voice of the dead that touches the cold living,
> Through the pale sunlight once more gravely speak.
> Tell me again, while the last leaves are falling:
> "Dear child, what has been once so interwoven
> Cannot be raveled, nor the gift ungiven."
>
> Now the dead move through all of us still glowing,
> Mother and child, lover and lover mated,
> Are wound and bound together and enflowing.
> What has been plaited cannot be unplaited—
> Only the strands grow richer with each loss
> And memory makes kings and queens of us.
>
> Dark into light, light into darkness, spin.
> When all the birds have flown to some real haven,

We who find shelter in the warmth within,
Listen, and feel new-cherished, new-forgiven,
As the lost human voices speak through us and blend
Our complex love, our mourning without end.[2]

Lighting the Candles

Let us light a candle in memory of someone who has died and share something about that person. *(Candle lighting and sharing)*

Reading: "Women Who Bear the Pain Over Life That Is Wasted in War" by Elizabeth Padillo-Olesen

Life is conceived in a womb
Protected in a seeming crystal bowl
Blood, love and hope are mingled together
to let this life behold the dawn.

But a sudden flash of light
dropped out of arrogance and might
tranforms this valuable being
into ashes of smoke, if not into
the crippled, and wounded
invalids thoughout their lives.

How the women groan!
How the mothers die a thousand deaths!
When life that is nurtured
from womb to the dawn of light
is shattered in a wasteland.[3]

Crystal Sharing

Crystals are believed to magnify, store, and focus energy. Regarded in Japan as symbols of eternity, they are used to transmit and direct energy. Let us pass this crystal around in silence and connect with the energy of loved ones who have gone before us. *(Sharing)*

Reading: "Retrospect in the Kitchen," by Maxine Kumin

After the funeral I pick
forty pounds of plums from your tree
Earth Wizard, Limb Lopper
and carry them by DC 10
three thousand miles to my kitchen

and stand at midnight—nine o'clock
your time—on the fourth day of your death
putting some raveled things unsaid between us
       into the boiling pot
of cloves, cinnamon, sugar.

Love's royal color
the burst purple fruit bob up.[4]

Song: "Breaths," by Sweet Honey in the Rock

Refrain:
Listen more often to things than to beings *(Repeat)*
'Tis the ancestors' prayer when the fire's voice is heard.
'Tis the ancestors' prayer in the voice of the waters.

Those who have died have never, never left.
The dead are not under the earth.
They are in the rustling leaves,
They are in the growing woods,
They are in the crying babes,
They are in the morning light.
The dead are not under the earth.

(Refrain)

Those who have died have never, never left.
The dead have a pact with the living.
They are in the woman's breast,

They are in the waiting child,
They are with us in the home,
They are with us in the ground.
The dead have a pact with the living.

(Refrain)[5]

Spiral Dance Meditation

(One woman starts the group in a spiral dance in silence. After a minute
she says:)

As you spiral, be with death and your own mortality. Focus on
something that is ending, or dying, or needs to die in you. (Pause)

Now go deep into the well of your being and get in touch with
something you would like to bring into being through the power
of your own intention, through the power of your own will. This
could be a new attitude, a new quality of being. It could be something concrete that you would like to manifest in your own life: a
change in relationship or a new understanding about yourself.

Get in touch with something that through your own power
you can make happen for yourself, and ask the Wise Woman,
Wisdom Sophia, the Holy One to help you. (Pause)

Ask her to give you something that will help you bring this
into being. And just allow any image or imaging to emerge. Accept
what she gives as it is given, without thought. (Pause)

And now, allow yourself to return. Return to consciousness.
Be present here with the gift or gifts that the Wise Woman has
given you. (Pause)

Reflection

Power moves through all of us. Endings and deaths, beginnings
and newness, mark life's cycles. Let us share whatever we wish
from our spiral dance. Share what intention you got in touch
with, what gift you received, or what insights you gained. (Sharing)

Blessing Food and Drink

(*The leader picks up the basket of bread, fruits, and nuts, and the glass of cider and says:*) Let us bless this food and drink in honor of ancestors.

> Blessed are you, Holy One of our Ancestors,
> For you give us our daily food and drink
> To connect us with the Communion of Saints.

Let us eat and drink, remembering our ancestors.

Blessing One Another

As we spiraled into the center of death and dying, let us now spiral into life and new beginnings. (*This time the spiral dance has a lively feel to it.*)

Song: "Sisters' Spiral," by Colleen Fulmer

(*This is a two-part circular canon.*)

> Spiraling, spiraling circle of Wisdom
> Sisters together a body of praise.
>
> Born of Earth her rhythms, cycles
> Love that's flowing from ancient of days.[6]

Sending Forth

As we go home tonight, go carefully and cautiously. The spirits are with us in a special way these days. Pay attention to your dreams. The veil between life and death is very thin.

> May your dreams connect you with loved ones.
> May your loved ones connect you to your power.
> May your power connect you to your mortality.

Let us open our circle.

NOTES

1. From Fulmer, *Dancing Sophia's Circle*.

2. In May Sarton, *Collected Poems 1930–1993* (New York: W. W. Norton, 1993), 185.

3. In Katsuno-Ishii and Orteza, eds., *Of Rolling Waters and Roaring Wind*, 43.

4. Maxine Kumin, "Retrospect in the Kitchen, from In Memoriam P. W. Jr., 1920–1980," from Maxine Kumin, *Selected Poems 1960–1990* (New York: W. W. Norton, 1996).

5. "Breaths," lyrics adapted from the poem "Breaths" by Birago Diop, music by Ysaye M. Barnwell © 1980 Barnwell's Notes Publishing, Washington, DC. Permission granted from Ysaye M. Barnwell. From Sweet Honey in the Rock, *Good News* © 1981, Flying Fish Records. Audio recording.

6. From Fulmer, *Dancing Sophia's Circle*.

partfour

WINTER *renewing the earth*

All things shall be well . . .
You shall see for yourself that all
manner of things shall be well.

— Julian of Norwich,
Revelation of Love

Then I saw a new heaven and a new earth.

— Revelation 21:1

The best remedy, for those who are afraid,
lonely, or unhappy is to go outside, somewhere
where they can be alone with the heavens,
nature, and God. Because only then does one
feel that all is as it should be and that God
wishes to see people happy, amidst the simple
beauty of nature. As long as this exists, and it
certainly always will, I know that then there
will always be comfort for every sorrow. . . .

—Anne Frank,
Diary of Anne Frank

Winter brings sweet darkness and chilling cold. We see the stark trees and barren lands, hear the quiet and silence, smell fires burning, touch the snow, feel the blustery wind, and taste steaming soup to warm us inside. This is a time to lie fallow. The spirits of the ancestors knew the power of darkness and hibernation, the sacredness of death and rebirth. The darkness, dormancy, and silent beauty of winter offer time for another vision. It is time to examine mortality. Mysteries lie in darkness. Solitude brings new dreams from the silence, the waiting, the time apart.

Winter invites a long journey inward to draw on natural resources and strength. The starkness of the environment can bring clarity. The structure of the tree and the shape of the land are revealed as they are freed from vegetation. We participate with the Earth in the sacred cycle: death preparing for rebirth, emptying to make space for the new. We rest and hibernate. We ponder and dream, as darkness turns into new life.

The ecofeminist liturgies in this section focus the themes of dreaming, death, rest, regeneration, examining mortality, hibernation, renewal. They use the symbols of candles, bonfires, Christmas tree, electric lights, evergreen wreaths, Yule log, grass seed. They urge us to heal the Earth in winter by caring for inside house plants, shoveling snow, repairing tools, making homemade holiday presents, using worn-out clothing to make a quilt, buying a live Christmas tree and planting it in the yard, using cat-box litter or sand (not salt) on icy sidewalks, refraining from purchasing items made from animals. Use them as models to celebrate the winter festivals of (approximately) December 21 (June 21), winter solstice; Chanukah; Advent; December 25, Christmas; December 26, Kwanzaa; January 1, New Year's Day; February 2, Brigid's Day, Imbloc, Candlemas.

fifteen

WINTER SOLSTICE AS FROM THE WOMB OF NIGHT

Life comes out of darkness. The winter solstice is the solar new year. Seasonal changes of winter are governed by the waning of the power of the sun that has reached its farthest distance from the equator. Daylight has waned and the night is longest at this midwinter. Each generation and almost every culture celebrate calling the sun from the womb of night. The winter solstice, on about December 21 (June 21), is marked by many festivals whose imagery is light: lighting a menorah, a Christmas tree, candles of Dewali, and bonfires. Each festival beseeches the sun to return again.

This winter solstice liturgy celebrates Chanukah, Kwanzaa, and Christmas. In it participants will light and dedicate Chanukah candles to peace, Kwanzaa candles to the power of community and overcoming racism, and the Advent/Christmas candles to peace on Earth.

Preparation

Place a Chanukah menorah, a Kwanzaa kinara, an Advent wreath, and a variety of candles on the altar table. The chanukia is a special menorah for Chanukah, with eight candles and a ninth for lighting—the sham-mis—which is usually placed in the tallest spot on the chanukia. The ki-nara contains three green candles, one black candle in the middle, and three red candles. The Advent wreath is a circle with four candles to represent the four Sundays of Advent. Protestants often use four white candles, and add a fifth candle in the center of the wreath as the Christ candle that is lit at Christmas. Catholics usually choose three purple candles and one pink for the third Sunday, Gaudete. Have ready a cup with water for the liba-tion. Bring instrumental flute music that invites reflection.

Call to Gather

Welcome to our celebration, "Winter Solstice as from the Womb of Night." This is the season of the winter solstice. Falling on ap-proximately December 21 in the northern hemisphere (June 21 in the southern) this is the longest night of the year, the night when darkness triumphs and yet gives way and changes into light. The winter solstice is marked by many festivals whose imagery is light. Tonight we name four of them: the communal festivals of the winter solstice, Chanukah, Kwanzaa, and Christmas. We recall them to remember that generation after generation calls the sun from the womb of night. Let us take a moment to ready ourselves to tell winter solstice stories.

Naming the Circle

What do you think of when you hear the words "From the Womb of Night"? *(Pause)* Share with us your name and your reflection. *(Sharing)*

TELLING WINTER SOLSTICE STORIES

Winter solstice, about December 21 (June 21), marks the return of the sun goddesses. In ancient times people commemorated the birth of the sun goddesses Lucina and Athar by lighting a yule log and burning it for seven days. In Anatolia, an evergreen tree, symbol of life amidst apparent death, was hung with the fleece of a ram. The fleece contained fat, seeds of wheat, and grapes. Prayers for health and abundance were said to the goddess Anat. Pine boughs have long been used during the solstice season, as have mistletoe, holly, and ivy.

In Japan, winter solstice marked the return of the sun goddess Amaterasu Omikami from her cave retreat. An eight-sided mirror was hung in a tree, so that she would see her own image and be lured out, thus renewing the brilliance of the sun. In early Rome, a woman-only festival for the Bona Dea, a goddess of healing, ensured prosperity and well-being for the coming year. In Scandinavia, twelve days around solstice were the holiday of Hulda or Holle, the goddess associated with spinning, weaving, and the cultivation of flax. Today many women worldwide celebrate winter solstice festivals to honor the Great Goddess.

Kindling the Lights

Tonight we light the first candle to kindle the winter solstice lights.

I light this candle to bring into this place the lights of the winter solstice, the power of the goddesses, the hope that in the new year women will be respected. (*Light a large candle.*)

Gathering Music

(*Play instrumental flute music.*)

TELLING THE CHANUKAH STORY

Chanukah is a Jewish feast of dedication that symbolizes steadfastness under oppression. It proclaims, "A great miracle occurred here."

The celebration has as one of its rituals the lighting of the eight-branched menorah, the chanukia. Each night another candle is lit until all are burning on the eighth night. The festival lasts for eight days to commemorate the eight days that the oil lamp burned to purify the temple after the Maccabees took it back.

The reclaiming of the temple by the Jews meant that their other rituals could be celebrated. This ritual symbolizes the nature of faith—that it will grow as long as there are those who will remember the stories and dedicate themselves to God.

Kindling the Lights

Tonight we light one candle to anticipate the first night of Chanukah, which is on the twenty-fifth day of the Hebrew month of Kislev. (*Light the shammis and from it the candle(s) that are appropriate for the date of your celebration, adapting the words as necessary.*)

I light this Chanukah candle to bring into this place the lights of Chanukah, the power of dedication, the hope that the new year will be dedicated to peace.

Blessing

Baruch atta hashem, elohaynu melek haolam,
asher kidshanu bemitzvotav
vetzivanu lehadlik ner shel Chanukah.

Blessed are you, Holy Creator,
For you give us this Chanukah light of dedication
to guide our ways.

Song: "This Little Light of Mine," traditional

This little light of mine, I'm gonna let it shine. (*Repeat*)
Let it shine, let it shine, let it shine.

Everywhere I go, I'm gonna let it shine. (*Repeat*)
Let it shine, let it shine, let it shine.

Throughout this solstice time, I'm gonna let it shine. (*Repeat*)
Let it shine, let it shine, let it shine.

Litany of Dedication

Let us recall the enlightenment gained through the lives of dedicated women.

LEADER: Blessed is Ruth, who dedicated herself to the God of Naomi, her mother-in-law.

RESPONSE: Dedicated be their lives.

LEADER: Blessed is Deborah, whose dedication to God brought her to leadership as judge among her people.

RESPONSE: Dedicated be their lives.

LEADER: Blessed is Hannah Senech, who wrote, "Blessed is the match consumed in kindling flame."

RESPONSE: Dedicated be their lives.

LEADER: Blessed is the woman who relishes her own company.

RESPONSE: Dedicated be their lives.

LEADER: Blessed are the old women who know the freedom of tears and the wisdom of laughter.

RESPONSE: Dedicated be their lives.

LEADER: Blessed is the Earth, the mother of us all.

RESPONSE: Dedicated be their lives.

LEADER: Blessed are the women who protect life on the planet.

RESPONSE: Dedicated be their lives.

LEADER: Blessed are . . . who else do we name? Tell us and we will respond.

Reflection

Let us reflect silently for a minute on the following question: To what do I dedicate myself? *(Pause)*

Song

Hum "This Little Light of Mine"

TELLING THE KWANZAA STORY

Kwanzaa is a unique American holiday that pays tribute to the rich cultural roots of Americans born of African ancestry. It is celebrated from December 26 through January 1.

Kwanzaa comes from the Swahili phrase "ya Kwanza," which means first fruits and refers to the first harvest celebrations in many African countries. This festival is based on seven fundamental principles, which are referred to as the *Nguzo Saba:* unity, *Umoja* (oo-MOH-ja); self-determination, *Kuujichagalia* (koo-ji-chah-goo-LEE-ah); collective work and responsibility, *Ujima* (oo-JEE-mah); cooperative economics, *Ujamaa* (oo-jah-MAH); purpose, *Nia* (NEE-ah); creativity, *Kuumba* (koo-OOM-bah); and faith, *Imani* (ee-MAH-nee).

This feast is "a time, a chance and challenge to turn inward and then outward to enjoy in still another way the beauties of being together, in the same group, extended family and organization, sharing the same values, interests, and aspirations, engaged in a commitment to the same struggle" (United Black Community of Washington, D.C.).

One of the rituals of Kwanzaa is the lighting of seven candles on successive evenings, beginning with the black candle, then alternating lighting from left to right. Each candle represents one of seven principles that are the foundation of African American life.

Kindling the Lights

Tonight we light one candle to anticipate the first night of Kwanzaa, which is December 26.

(Light the candle(s) appropriate for the date of your celebration, adapting the words accordingly.)

I light this candle to bring into this place the lights of Kwanzaa, the power of community, the hope that in the new year we will overcome racism.

Song: "Come and Go with Me to That Land," traditional, adapted

> Come and go with me to that land, come and go with me to
> that land.
> Come and go with me to that land where I'm bound. (*Repeat*)

> Umoja in that land, Umoja in that land.
> Umoja in that land where I'm bound. (*Repeat*)

> (*Repeat, using the following for each new verse.*) Kuujichagalia . . .
> Ujima . . . Ujamaa . . . Nia . . . Kuumba . . . Imani . . .[1]

Sharing the Libation

It is an African tradition on all special occasions to pour a libation
in remembrance of the ancestors. Tonight we pour water, which
holds the essence of life, from our communal cup in the direction
of the four winds: south, east, north, and west. (*The leader pours the
water.*) Please say after me our Libation Litany:

> For Africa, cradle of civilization. (*Echo*)
> For the ancestors and their courageous spirits. (*Echo*)
> For the elders who teach wisdom. (*Echo*)
> For the young, who are the promise of tomorrow. (*Echo*)
> For those who work against racism. (*Echo*)
> For Umoja, the principle of unity. (*Echo*)
> For the Creator, who provides all things. (*Echo*)

Let us sip from this cup, remembering. (*Pass the cup of libation
around the group.*)

Reflection

Let us share with another person how we participate in the
African American struggle for liberation. (*Sharing*)

Song: "We Shall Overcome," traditional
(*Remember to cross your wrists, right over left, and hold the hands of the
people next to you as you sing.*)

TELLING THE CHRISTMAS STORY

Christmas celebrates the coming of God into human history. Each December 25 Christians remember how Blessed Mary gave birth to Jesus, the God of Peace, who is Miriam's Child and Sophia's Prophet. The lessons from the scripture readings for this season are filled with visions of the establishment of justice and right relation on Earth.

Advent is a time of anticipation and preparation for the birth of light, the birth of the light of the world and the son (sun) of God. Advent means "coming." Starting on the Sunday nearest to November 30 and containing the four Sundays before Christmas day, it marks the beginning of the church year. Lighting another candle on the Advent wreath signals each of the four weeks of Advent.

Kindling the Lights

Tonight we light one candle on the Advent wreath to begin a new year. (*Light the number of candles that are appropriate for the date of your celebration, adapting the words accordingly.*)

I light this Advent wreath to bring into this place the light of Advent and Christmas, the flames of justice and right relation on Earth, the hope that the coming year will be one of world peace.

Song: "Rejoice! Rejoice!" tune "O Come, O Come, Emmanuel"

O Come, O come, Emmanuel,
And ransom captive Israel.
That mourns in lonely exile here
Until a Liberator is near.

Refrain:
Rejoice! Rejoice! Our freedom is at hand.
The Dawn of Justice shines upon the land.

Come now, dear friends, for Advent time is here;
It's time to cast out doubt and crippling fear—

For presently, before our wondering eyes,
This season will bring forth its own surprise.

(Refrain)[2]

Reading: Adapted from "The Work of Christmas," by Howard
Thurman

When the song of the angels is stilled,
When the star in the sky is gone,
When the [wise women and men] are home,
When the shepherds are back with their flock,
The work of Christmas begins:
To find the lost,
To heal the broken,
To feed the hungry,
To release the prisoner,
To rebuild the nations,
To bring peace among [people],
To make music in the heart.[3]

Song: "Rejoice! Rejoice!"

O come, O Wisdom, sister of us all,
Prepare our ears to hear a wondrous call.
To us the path of knowledge show,
And teach us in your ways to go.

(Refrain)

Let us together ponder how we may
Initiate a new and better day.
In numbers we are strong, our faith is great;
No more delay lest justice come too late.

(Refrain)

Reflection

Let us share a Christmas concern or wish with one another. *(Sharing)*

TELLING OTHER WINTER SOLSTICE STORIES

There are other candles around this room that you may want to light or ones that you may want to blow out. Tell us other stories that celebrate the winter solstice and kindle the lights. *(Sharing stories)*

Blessing One Another

Gathered in the womb of this night, let us form a circle shoulder to shoulder. Close your eyes and feel the power of the darkness around us and within us. Call forth from within you your creativity and your healing powers. Filled with the power of the winter solstice, let us bless one another. *(Blessing)*

Sending Forth

Filled with the power of the winter solstice,
Let us dedicate ourselves to steadfastness under oppression,
Let us enjoy the beauties of being together,
And let us bring justice, peace, and right relations to the Earth.
Let us go forth and cherish the darkness.
Let us now open our circle.

Song

(Sing a medley of holiday songs that are familiar to your group.)

NOTES

1. "Come and Go with Me to That Land," adapted from the traditional by Diann Neu.

2. "Rejoice! Rejoice!" words adapted from the traditional by Diann Neu.

3. In Howard Thurman, *The Mood of Christmas and Other Celebrations* (Richmond, IN: Friends United Press, 1985), 23.

sixteen

BLESSED BE THE NEW YEAR

The New Year is a season when spirits of hope and change intermingle. This divide between what has been and what is to come invites us to contemplate new beginnings and articulate farewells.

This liturgy invites the Great Spirit of Hope to bless this holy season. Use it for individual reflection or invite a friend or several to join you in giving it expression.

Preparation

Pick your favorite candle and put it in a special place. Or gather many significant candles and arrange them to please yourself. Choose a quiet time of the day for your lighting. Put on music if you wish. Rest your body in a comfortable place and relax. Your candle(s) joined with those of others around the world illuminate new hopes, and dispel old fears.

Centering

(Light your candle.)
This is the season of hope!
    Let the Spirit of Hope surround me (us).
        Let my (our) spirit rise to bless this New Year.

Blessing

O Great Spirit of Hope, blessed be your holy seasons.
    Blessed be this season when we move to a New Year.
    Blessed be this magical time for new beginnings
        and fond farewells.
    Blessed be this "crack between worlds" that we encounter
        at the New Year.
    Blessed be this threshold of transition between inside
        and outside.
    Blessed be this transformation when spirits of hope
        and change gather.
    Blessed be this passage from past securities to uncharted
        uncertainties.
    Blessed be this shifting of emotions.
    Blessed be this letting go of old hurts and pains.
    Blessed be this reliable balancing act of nature.
    Blessed be this rededication of values and meaning in life.
    Blessed be . . . *(add others)*
O Great Spirit of Hope, blessed be your holy seasons.

Reflection

What are the transitions that I experience as a new season of a new year dawns?

What new goals for health, social change, and sharpening my focus do I set for myself?

What actions will I take to heal the Earth?

(*Pause to reflect, journal, converse, draw, or dance as you wish.*)

Closure

This is the season of hope!

Let the Spirit of Hope surround me.

Let my (our) spirit rise to bless this New Year.

Blow out the candle(s), knowing you can rekindle one or all at any time.

seventeen

ALL SHALL BE WELL AGAIN

Winter can be difficult. It often seems more darkness than light, a time for withdrawal and hibernation rather than community. During winter, faith may be tested to the core and spiritual roots can deepen. If a winter is especially hard, many are ready to bid it farewell as soon as possible.

In this liturgy participants say goodbye to winter and welcome the renewal of spring. They light candles and ring bells to let the winter go. They plant bulbs and reflect on the springtime blooms that promise "all shall be well again."

Preparation

Place a bell, nine small candles, crocus and daffodil bulbs, containers with rocks or soil, and a pitcher of water on a central symbol table. (You can grow bulbs in the house in winter by placing them either in a special bulb vase that uses water, or in a container with rocks and water or soil and water.)

Call to Gather

(One lights a candle. Adapt these words to your own context.)

Winter ice and snow remind us that a thaw and a greening are around the bend. As the crocuses ready to peek out from the Earth and the birds return to singing, their promise invites us to pay attention to the spring renewal that will soon happen around us. Yes, it is time to let go of winter and remember that all shall be well again. This is what we celebrate.

Naming the Circle

(Another lights a candle.)

Let us create our circle by speaking our names and saying, "All shall be well again." *(Naming)*

Letting Go of Winter

(The reader lights a candle.)

We need to let go of winter, all forms of winter, so all can be well again. Please respond by saying, "Go, winter, go."

LEADER: Depart, deadening spirit of winter, from our lives.

RESPONSE: **Go, winter, go.**

LEADER: Be gone, all slippery ice, slushy sleet, dangerous snow, and piercing winds.

RESPONSE: **Go, winter, go.**

LEADER: Be gone, all ice, sleet, and cold in our personal lives: snide remarks, judgmental statements, cruel jokes, nasty gossip, untruthful comments.

RESPONSE: Go, winter, go.

LEADER: Be gone, times of loneliness and harshness.

RESPONSE: Go, winter, go.

LEADER: Be gone . . . Tell us, beginning with "Be gone," what you wish to let go of. We will respond, "Go, winter, go." (*Wishes and responses*)

LEADER: Hear our prayer and go, O Spirit of Winter. Depart from our neighborhoods and from our lives for another year. Be gone. Be gone. Be gone.

Chant: "All Shall Be Well," by Rufino Zaragoza

> All shall be well.
> All shall be well.
> All manner of things shall be well.[1]

Reading: "All Winter Long," Native American song
(*The reader lights a candle.*)

> All winter long
> behind every thunder
> guess what we heard!
> —behind every thunder
> the song
> of a bird,
> a trumpeting bird.

> All winter long
> beneath every snowing
> guess what we saw!
> —beneath every snowing
> a thaw
> and a growing,
> a greening and growing.

Where did we run
beyond gate and guardsman?
Guess, if you can!
—all winter long
we ran
to the sun,
the dance of the sun!²

Chant

All shall be well.
All shall be well.
All manner of things shall be well.

Reading: "A Light Exists in Spring," by Emily Dickinson

(*The reader lights a candle.*)

A light exists in Spring
Not present on the Year
At any other period—
When March is scarcely here

A Color stands abroad
On Solitary Fields
That Science cannot overtake
But Human Nature feels.
It waits upon the Lawn,
It shows the furthest Tree
Upon the furthest Slope you know
It almost speaks to you.

Then as Horizons step
Or Noons report away
Without the Formula of sound
It passes and we stay—

A quality of loss
Affecting our Content
As Trade had suddenly encroached
Upon a Sacrament.[3]

Chant

All shall be well.
All shall be well.
All manner of things shall be well.

Reading: Psalm 148, adapted by Diann Neu

(The reader lights a candle and says:) Let us read this antiphonally.

SIDE ONE: Alleluia!
   Praise Wisdom Sophia.
   Praise her from the heavens; praise her in all places.
   Praise her, all you angels; praise her, all you Earthlings.
   Praise her, sun and moon; praise her, stars and galaxies.

ALL: **Praise the name of Wisdom Sophia!**

SIDE TWO: For she loved and they were created.
   And she established them forever and ever.
   What Wisdom Sophia desires and decrees will never pass away.

ALL: **Praise the name of Wisdom Sophia!**

SIDE ONE: Praise Wisdom Sophia from the Earth,
      you sea creatures and deep waters.
   Fire and hail, snow and frost, and stormy winds fulfill her will.
   Mountains and hills, fruit trees and all cedars,
   Living creatures and all cattle, reptiles and flying birds.

ALL: **Praise the name of Wisdom Sophia!**

SIDE TWO: Activists and leaders, healers and teachers, praise her.
   All peoples of the Earth, praise her!
   Children and elders, young and old, women and men.

ALL: **Praise the name of Wisdom Sophia!**

SIDE ONE: Praise the name of Wisdom Sophia.
> Let her be exalted and honored,
> For her glory fills both heaven and Earth!
> She acts for all her people—

ALL: **Praise the name of Wisdom Sophia!**

SIDE TWO: Let her faithful ones praise her!
> Let her daughters and sons praise her.
> Let the people close to her praise her, singing "Alleluia" forever!

ALL: **Praise the name of Wisdom Sophia!**
> **Alleluia! Alleluia! Alleluia!**

Chant

> All shall be well.
> All shall be well.
> All manner of things shall be well.

Reflection

(The leader lights a candle and says:)

Winter and spring represent the seasons of our lives. This year, what is that winter to which I am saying goodbye? What is the springtime for which I hope? What bulbs do I want to bloom in my life so all can be well again? Let us take a few minutes for quiet reflection, then I will invite us to plant bulbs and share with one another our reflections. *(Reflecting, planting, sharing)*

Blessing the Bulbs

(The leader lights a candle and says:) Hold your bulb and pray after me:

> Source of Life, One who brings forth crocuses and daffodils
> *(Echo)*
> Praise to you for blessing the Earth with beauty. *(Echo)*

Renew us with flowing water *(Echo)*
Singing birds and spring light. *(Echo)*
All shall be well again. *(Echo)*
All shall be well again. *(Echo)*
All shall be well again. *(Echo)*
Amen. Blessed be. Let it be so. *(Echo)*

Chant

All shall be well.
All shall be well.
All manner of things shall be well.

Sending Forth

(One lights a candle.)

Let us go forth to notice the renewal of the Earth.
May our eyes be open to the bulbs peeking out of the soil.
May our ears hear the singing birds.
May our feet touch the Earth gently.

Let us go forth to return blessings to the Earth, sea, and sky.
May our Earth be renewed.
May our waters be clean.
May our air be pure.
May all be well again.
Amen. Blessed be. Let it be so.

Let us now open our circle.

NOTES

1. From *Light of Christ* ©1988, Oregon Catholic Press. Audio recording.

2. In Roberts and Amidon, *Earth Prayers,* 327.

3. Poem 812 is reprinted by permission of the publishers and the Trustees of Amherst College from Thomas H. Johnson, ed., *The Poems of Emily Dickinson* (Cambridge, MA: Belknap Press of Harvard University, 1951, 1955, 1979), by the President and Fellows of Harvard College.

eighteen

GREEN POWER RETURNS

Spring returns each year, from generation to generation. Festivals during this time invite participants to notice the light that is reawakening. They celebrate the passage of power between the Earth and the sun that begins the germination and regeneration of nature. Brigid's Day, Candlemas, and Imbloc, February 1 (August 1) are traditional feasts that signal the end of the old year and the prelude to the new.

This liturgy celebrates the renewal of spring by honoring the spirits of the east, south, west, and north for returning ever-greening life to planet Earth. It invites participants to renew the Earth by scattering grass seeds, reflecting on personal ever-greening life, and committing to an action to save planet Earth.

Preparation

Take some grass seeds. Be ready to plant them in a pot on your windowsill, scatter them at your doorstep, or broadcast them in your yard. Have water handy. Invite a friend or several to join your "sowing" circle, if you wish. Gather in silence, sing, or play music.

Centering

This is the season when light reawakens.
Let the Creator of All Life surround you.
Pause and give thanks for the return of spring.

Chant: "The Four Element Chant," by Joy Willow

In my soul, the sun is shining,
In my heart, the flowing stream,
In my breath, the air of mountains,
In my body, Mother Earth.[1]

(Scatter the seeds.)

Prayer

Praise to you, Creator of All Things Living, for the green life that you return to the Earth. Praise to you for the restless power of the wind, the warm energy of the sun, the steady flow of gentle rain, and the spirit of living things as they return to Earth. How many and wonderful are your works, O Living Creator. We honor and praise you now and forever. Amen. Blessed be. Let it be so.

Invocation

(Pray, and if comfortable and convenient, face each direction.)

Spirit of the East, Winds of the Air Cycle,
You breathe in oxygen to awaken each cell;
You breathe out carbon dioxide to the grasses.
Return ever-greening life to planet Earth.

Spirit of the South, Metabolism of the Fire Cycle,
You touch seeds with sun that fuels all life;
You embrace the world with energy.
Return ever-greening life to planet Earth.

Spirit of the West, Flow of the Water Cycle,
Blood, lymph, mucus, sweat, tears;
You make powerful rivers run.
Return ever-greening life to planet Earth.

Spirit of the North, Creation of the Earth Cycle,
You replace each cell in the human body every seven years,
You contain all nourishment, all verdancy,
        all germinating power.
Return ever-greening life to planet Earth.

(Water the grass seeds.)

Reflection

What ever-greening life do I need to protect within myself this spring? What actions will I take to save the water, the earth, the air, and the energy supplies for the life of planet Earth? *(Take time to walk outside or do something that puts you in touch with nature.)*

Blessing: "May Beauty Be," traditional Navajo chant

May beauty be before me. *(Stretch hands in front)*
May beauty be behind me. *(Stretch hands behind)*
May beauty be below me. *(Stretch hands down to feet)*
May beauty be above me. *(Raise hands toward sky)*
May beauty be all around me. *(Turn around, with
        outstretched arms)*
In beauty it was begun. *(Hug yourself)*
In beauty it is finished. *(Stretch hands out in front)*

Chant: "The Four Element Chant"

> In my soul, the sun is shining,
> In my heart, the flowing stream,
> In my breath, the air of mountains,
> In my body, Mother Earth.

Closing

> This is the season when the light reawakens.
> Let the Creator of All Life surround you.
> Pause and give thanks for the return of spring.

NOTES

1. Reprinted from Middleton, *Songs for Earthlings,* 114.

epilogue

RETURN BLESSINGS

*"A new vision—a new life for present and
future generations, and for our fellow creatures
on earth—in which praxis and theory are respected
and preserved can be found only in the survival
struggles of grassroots movements."*

— Vandava Shiva, *Ecofeminism*

The ecofeminist liturgies in this book call us to return blessings to
creation by paying attention to ecofriendly living, and acting in
Earth-centered ways. They encourage us to live an eco-spirituality
that does justice so that the Earth can survive.

Women worldwide are creating models of community and
practice to heal the Earth and to insure the future of the cosmos.
They are developing and sharing with one another methods, tech-
nology, and philosophy about energy efficiency, Earth-friendly living, and ecofeminist liturgies. They challenge us to unlearn the
throwaway culture of the twentieth century and change our
lifestyles to reflect and enable a sustainable future for all creation.
Together we are searching for an ecologically sound, just, nonex-

ploitative, noncolonial, and self-sustaining society that respects, not destroys, nature.

Women around the world are modeling ecofriendly living, taking the lead to protect nature, and reclaiming Earth-based spirituality.

Con-spirando, Santiago, Chile. This collective has been weaving a network of women throughout Latin America who are interested in feminist theology, spirituality, and ecofeminism. It publishes a quarterly and holds women's rituals. Mary Judith Ress, a member of the collective, describes their rituals:

> Here in Santiago, we at Con-spirando are drawn to hold our rituals outside under the trees—even in the winter when we are "sandwiched" in a cloud cover of poisonous gas. We are pulled to dance and chant to the beat of the drum as we try to pick up the rhythms in the earth—the *Pachamama*—and in our own bodies. We are attracted to the modern *machis* and *curanderas* walking the streets, old aunts and grandmothers who tell us what to do for our kids' asthma or for our own aches and pains—who seem to offer balm for the spirit as well as the body. The sense of interconnectedness present in the Mapuche and Aymara traditions, of the need to give back to the earth what we take, rings so true to us and we hunger to put it in practice.[1]

The earth, the air, the fire, the water return!

EarthConnection, Cincinnati, Ohio, USA. Paula Gonzalez, founding director of this nonprofit solar program sponsored by the Sisters of Charity, describes the unique EarthConnection building (a 3,900-square-foot facility heated and lit basically with solar energy). It is "a place where average suburbanites and city dwellers can learn . . . about solar design construction, water conservation, and other measures to help us all live more lightly on this magnificent

Earth, as well as to probe the deep spiritual meaning of eco-sensitive living." In this group's quarterly publication Paula reports the excitement of starting up their first solar collectors. She writes:

> It works! It works! This was the delighted cry that we at EC danced around shouting on August 16, 1994. Randy started up the solar collectors and we watched as the summer sunshine began to "pour into the ground" in the insulated underground storage system surrounding the building. Each sunny day we record temperatures and smile as we look forward to using this "stored sunshine" in January! This historic event brings me to reach out to all out there who are serious about joining the paradigm shift represented by what is happening here. We are replacing significant amounts of fossil fuel by "connecting" Earth's free gifts: FIRE is being carried by WATER into the EARTH to be recovered later by warming the AIR in the EC building. Someday, when we can afford photovoltaic (PV) panels, the sun will provide for most of our routine electrical needs; and when our cistern system is built, rain will become our water source![2]

The earth, the air, the fire, the water return!

Igorot women, Cordillera, Philippines. These indigenous women engage in subsistence agriculture and do rituals to thank or appease nature spirits and ancestors. Their rituals coincide with agricultural cycles and the life-cycles: before planting and harvesting rice; during births, weddings, and deaths; and other times. When a woman gives birth, the placenta is buried in a carefully chosen place to make that land more valuable.

> The basic belief of the Igorots is that nature or the earth is a living thing and it has a spirit, just like all the living things in it. The rivers, mountains, trees, rice fields, and so

on, each has its own spirits. This is why it is important to live in harmony with nature.[3]

The earth, the air, the fire, the water return!

The Chipko Movement, India. Women in India have stopped men from cutting the sacred trees from their village for timber by clinging to the trees and hugging them. The first such record of resistance against the destruction of creation dates back to the 1730s; the more recent one was in early 1970. This song, sung by the Garhwahl women of the Chipko movement, is a homage to the protection of life:

> A fight for truth has begun
> At Sinsyaru Khala
> A fight for rights has begun
> At Malkot Thano
> Sister, it is a fight to protect
> Our mountains and forests.
> They give us life
> Embrace the life of the living trees and streams
> Clasp them to your hearts
> Resist the digging of mountains
> That brings death to our forests and streams
> A fight for life has begun
> At Sinsyaru Khala.

> —*Chamundeyi, Doon Valley*
> Inspired by the Chipko poet Ghanshayam "Shailan"[4]

The earth, the air, the fire, the water return!

The Greenbelt Movement, Kenya. This organization, founded by Professor Wangari Maathai, a leading feminist and ecological activist, mobilizes women at the grassroots level to participate in an aggressive reforestation program.

The organization aims not only at reclaiming the quality of the land through planting trees, it also aims at reclaiming women's power by planting afresh the sense of self-confidence and pride in themselves nurtured in precolonial times by many African societies. This reclaimed self-confidence makes women better equipped to fight the multi-headed monster of injustice in Africa.[5]

The earth, the air, the fire, the water return!

Greening of Harlem Coalition, Harlem, New York, USA. Bernadette Cozart, a professional gardener, founded the coalition in 1989 to help people to take back their own neighborhoods, transform rundown vacant lots in Harlem into flower gardens, and restore and revitalize existing green spaces. Bernadette has developed and worked on garden projects with young women at the School for Pregnant and Parenting Teens, prisoners on work release at Edgecomb Avenue Prison Facility, and drug addicts at the Addict Rehabilitation Center, as well as school children, senior citizens, AIDS patients, and the mentally ill. In an interview she says:

The first park that the Greening of Harlem Coalition decided to take back was Col. Charles Young Park at 143rd Street and Lenox Avenue. Everyone thought they were crazy because most people felt like you needed an Uzi just to walk into the area. Empty buildings next to the park had become crack houses. The place was one big drug supermarket. Prostitution was everywhere. The Coalition got the police to make regular sweeps until it became impossible for criminals to remain. As they moved out, Bernadette and her folk moved in. They did a big cleanup, getting rid of trash, broken glass, crack vials, and other drug paraphernalia. The Department of Parks and Recreation put in new playground equipment. Local residents helped to plant green spaces. With almost 5,600 tulips, they created the African Garden, one of the largest tulip gardens in Harlem.

The earth, the air, the fire, the water return!

These women model Earth-centered living that returns blessing. What do we learn from them about living in greater harmony
with the Earth? Their ecojustice projects focus five areas of Earth-
centered living that return blessings: beautification, recycling, energy use, land use, and spirituality.

Beautification of the environment fosters Earth-centered living and returns blessings.

To beautify the Earth:

Develop interesting and welcoming environments near buildings, entrances, and paths.

Reduce mowing and provide natural habitats for wildlife and
birds. Subsequent reduction of mowing results in substantial sav-
ings in the costs of fuel, machinery, and labor.

Garden in the city; reclaim vacant lots; take advantage of every
possible space to put trees, shrubbery, grass, vines. Imagine a graf-
fiti wall covered with flowering wisteria. Picture all the center di-
vides of thoroughfares blooming with daffodils. Think how colorful buildings would be with flower boxes full of petunias in their
windows. Imagine converting rooftops into food gardens.

Plant trees and ground cover. Ground cover restores land to
its natural appearance.

TREE FACTS:

- In fifty years one tree recycles more than $37,000 worth of
  water, provides $31,000 worth of erosion control, gives
  $62,000 worth of air pollution control, and produces
  $37,000 worth of oxygen;
- Two mature trees provide enough oxygen for a family of four;
- By cooling the air and ground around them, the shade from
  trees helps cool the Earth's temperature;
- Trees help prevent city flooding by catching raindrops and
  offsetting runoff caused by buildings and parking lots;

- Hospital patients heal faster and require shorter stays and less painkillers if room windows face trees;
- Well-placed trees help cut fossil-fuel consumption by decreasing air conditioning costs 10–50 percent and reducing heating costs 4–22 percent;
- Trees reduce "greenhouse effect" by absorbing CO_2. An acre of trees removes 2.6 tons of CO_2 per year;
- To remove a pound of CO_2: Planting a tree costs less than one cent, developing more energy efficient appliances costs about two and a half cents, and developing more fuel efficient cars costs about ten cents;
- Trees are good noise barriers, making a city and neighborhood quieter;
- Trees are the longest living and largest living organisms on Earth;
- A tree-line buffer between fields and streams removes most farming pollutants before they reach the water;
- People who plant trees get healthier, better looking, and richer, and have more friends (well, maybe that's stretching it a bit)—plant a tree and find out!

The earth, the air, the fire, the water return!

Recycling fosters Earth-centered living and returns blessings.

Compost: Put all kitchen wastes such as vegetable and fruit rinds, eggshells, coffee grounds, grass clippings, and leaves in a worm bed or a compost bin to be transformed into resources. I use my compost for plants.

Make worm beds: Worms produce their body weight in nutrient-rich castings. They reproduce bisexually. As their numbers increase, handfuls are transferred from the worm bed into newly dug vegetable beds where they tunnel around searching for the organic material they will transform into compost. They make openings in the soil through which air and water can enter more easily. I have been in city houses where worm beds live in the basement.

Recycle urine: Urine is a rich source of nitrogen which, when applied directly on a compost bin, helps to heat it up. Or, diluted five to one, it is a liquid fertilizer for trees or bushes. Coffee cans can be provided in bathrooms for the purpose of urine collection. When I lived in a group house with Carol Coston, she taught us to recycle urine onto the tomato plants and compost bins. After I recovered from my initial repulsion, I experienced an integrated connection among the Earth, my body, and the delicious tomatoes we ate throughout the Washington, D.C., summers.

Recycle: As waste disposal costs rise, recycling makes increasing economic and environmental sense. Collection bins for paper, plastic, glass, and cardboard make this easier.

Make and buy EarthStuff items: These unique "re-creations" are made from recycled or salvaged materials—things like a bird feeder made from discarded grape crates or a bird house made from scrap lumber or specialty cloth items fashioned from remnants. EarthConnections of Cincinnati has an EarthStore with EarthStuff products.

Wear cotton clothes when possible.

The earth, the air, the fire, the water return!

Less energy use fosters Earth-centered living and returns blessings.

Install deep-well supply pumps. Improvements to water supply and treatment facilities bring economic and environmental benefits. Deep-well pumps operate with greater capacity and efficiency and eliminate the need to use ground water to ensure an adequate water supply.

Decrease dependence on fossil fuels by making informed and responsible choices in the areas of transportation, heating, and other energy needs, and by employing renewable, nonpolluting energy sources when feasible. Use public transportation.

The earth, the air, the fire, the water return!

Conscientious land use fosters Earth-centered living and returns blessings.

Care for the grounds organically, without the use of chemical fertilizers, herbicides, or pesticides.

Establish "beautification areas" with walks and benches to enjoy the beauty of gardens.

Plan space for orchards to grow a variety of fruit trees.

The earth, the air, the fire, the water return!

Ecofeminist liturgies foster Earth-centered living and return blessings.

Sit in a chair and gaze at trees. Feel the interconnection.

Begin each day praying or chanting an invocation of creation, for example, "Earth my mother / Water my blood / Air my breath / Fire my spirit / All is One."

Create and celebrate liturgies to bring Earth-centered spirituality into harmony with actions on behalf of the beautiful planet.

Women of Sisterfarm in Welfare, Texas, USA, led by co-founders Carol Coston and Elise Garcia, ritualized the building of a compost pile in the Hildegard herb garden. One by one, the women in the circle surrounding the compost bin contributed something to the layering process—leaves, vegetable and fruit scraps, ashes, and more as the gathered sang and danced. Then, one woman watered it with a lovely English watering can.

This same group celebrated a house and land blessing. They started the ritual in the living room with a Spanish song about Earth blessings, then moved to the dining room where a Norwegian guest blessed them and all who would gather for future meals around the simple wooden table that was a Guatemalan vendor's table in an earlier life. An Irish kitchen blessing ensued, followed by a festive circling around the Esperanza Garden where the niche for Our Lady of Guadalupe and surrounding trees were festooned with Mexican colored streamers. As the blessing progressed around the property, women who had contributed "sweat equity" to a particular part of Sisterfarm led the prayer at that place.

RETURN BLESSINGS

These five areas of Earth-centered living are about transformation. By creating Earth-centered rituals, starting up the solar connectors, hugging trees, reforesting, or transforming rundown vacant lots into gardens, women are creating an act of power that returns blessings to the Earth.

How do you initiate this process in your life? You can start just about anywhere. You can start with recycling, with your means of transportation, with your diet and food-buying practices, with composting, with your relationships, with meditation, right livelihood, housing, gardening, conversation, liturgy—it is up to you. What seems easiest, most obvious, or most urgent to you? Start there.

Consider the eggplant and the earthworm. In gardening terms, the eggplant is a heavy feeder—it takes so many nutrients from the soil that, after it is harvested, additional phosphorous and potash must be returned, usually in the form of bone meal, wood ash, and compost. To return nitrogen to the soil, heavy givers must be planted—nitrogen-giving plants or legumes such as peas, beans, or alfalfa.

In global economic terms, it appears that those of us who live in the First World have a long history of being eggplants: relying on the natural resources of poorer countries to keep us supplied with our nutrients, and often depleting their ecological foundations as a result.

If we acted more like earthworms instead of being global egg-plants, we would go far toward sustaining a healthy web of life and creating alternative economic systems. As global earthworms, we would embody a key principle of organic gardening: we would be conscious, in all our activities, personal and institutional, of giving back to the Earth as much as, or more than, we took from it.

Let us return blessings to the Earth. Let us commit ourselves to Earth-centered living. Let us celebrate ecofeminist liturgies.

NOTES

1. Mary Judith Ress, "After Five Centuries of Mixings, Who Are We?" in Reuther, *Women Healing Earth*, 58.

2. Paula Gonzalez, *EC News* (Autumn 1994), 2.

3. Victoria Tauli-Corpuz, "Reclaiming Earth-based Spirituality," in Reuther, *Women Healing Earth*, 100–1.

4. Quoted in Vandana Shiva, *Staying Alive: Women, Ecology and Development*, (Delhi: Kali for Women, 1988), 210.

5. Teresia Hinga, "The Gikuyu Theology of Land," in Reuther, *Women Healing Earth*, 182.

BIBLIOGRAPHY

Collections of Feminist Prayers and Liturgies

Abbott, Margie, RSM. *Sparks of the Cosmos: Rituals for Seasonal Use.* Unley, South Australia: MediaCom Education, 2001.

Aldredge-Clanton, Jann. *Praying with Christ-Sophia.* Mystic, CT: Twenty-Third Publications, 1996.

Anderson, Virginia Cobb. *Prayers of Our Hearts in Word and Action.* New York: Crossroad, 1991.

Beben, Mary, and Bridget Mary Meehan. *Walking the Prophetic Journey: Eucharistic Liturgies for 21st Century Small Faith Communities.* Boulder: WovenWord Press, 1998.

Bowe, Barbara, Kathleen Hughes, Sharon Karam, and Carolyn Osiek, eds. *Silent Voices, Sacred Lives: Women's Readings for the Liturgical Year.* New York: Paulist Press, 1992.

Cady, Susan, Hal Taussig, and Marian Ronan. *Wisdom's Feast: Sophia in Study and Celebration.* San Francisco: Harper & Row, 1989.

Cherry, Kittredge, and Zalmon Sherwood, eds. *Equal Rites: Lesbian and Gay Worship, Ceremonies, and Celebrations.* Louisville: Westminster John Knox Press, 1995.

Con-spirando. *Cuadrno de Ritos.* Santiago, Chile: Colectivo Con-spirando, 1995.

Edelman, Marian Wright. *Guide My Feet: Prayers and Meditations on Loving and Working for Children.* Boston: Beacon Press, 1995.

Eiker, Diane, and Sapphire Eiker, eds. *Keep Simple Ceremonies.* Portland, ME: Astarte Shell Press, 1993.

Falk, Marcia. *The Book of Blessings: New Jewish Prayers for Daily Life, the Sabbath, and the New Moon Festival.* San Francisco: HarperCollins, 1996.

Grinnan, Jeanne Frinkman, Mary Rose McCarthy, Barbara S. Mitrano, and Rosalie Muschal-Reinhardt. *Sisters of the Thirteen Moons: Rituals Celebrating Women's Lives.* Webster, NY: The Prism Collective, 1997.

————. *Rituals for Women Coping with Breast Cancer.* Webster, NY: The Prism Collective, 2000.

Haydock, snjm, Kathy McFaul, and the Women of Weavers. *We Are Sisters: Prayer and Ritual for Women's Spirituality and Empowerment.* Seattle: Intercommunity Peace & Justice Center, 1996.

Henderson, J. Frank, ed. *Remembering the Women: Women's Stories from Scripture for Sundays and Festivals.* Chicago: Liturgy Training Publications, 1999.

Henry, Kathleen M. *The Book of Ours: Liturgies for Feminist People.* Jamaica Plain, MA: Alabaster Jar Liturgical Arts, 1993.

Katsuno-Ishii, Lynda, and Edna J. Orteza. *Of Rolling Waters and Roaring Wind: A Celebration of the Woman Song.* Geneva, Switzerland: WCC Publications, 2000.

Kirk, Martha Ann. *Celebrations of Biblical Women's Stories: Tears, Milk and Honey.* Kansas City, MO: Sheed and Ward, 1987.

Littell, Marcia Sachs, and Sharon Weissman Gutman, eds. *Liturgies on the Holocaust.* Valley Forge, PA: Trinity Press International, 1996.

Martensen, Jean, ed. *Sing Out New Visions.* Minneapolis: Augsburg Fortress, 1998.

McEwan, Dorothea, Pat Pinsent, Ianthe Pratt, and Veronica Seddon, eds. *Making Liturgy: Creating Rituals for Worship and Life.* Norwich, Norfolk, England: Canterbury Press, 2001.

Mitchell, Rosemary Catalano, and Gail Anderson Ricciuti. *Birthings and Blessings: Liberating Services for the Inclusive Church.* New York: Crossroad, 1991.

_____. *Birthings and Blessings II: More Liberating Worship Services for the Inclusive Church.* New York: Crossroad, 1993.

Morley, Janet. *All Desires Known: Inclusive Prayers for Worship and Meditation.* Harrisburg, PA: Morehouse Publishing, 1988, 1992.

National Sisters Vocation Conference. *Woman's Song.* Chicago: National Sisters Vocation Conference, 1986.

_____. *Woman's Song II.* Chicago: National Sisters Vocation Conference, 1987.

Neu, Diann L. *Women-Church Celebrations: Feminist Liturgies for the Lenten Season.* Silver Spring, MD: WATERworks Press, 1985.

_____. *Women and the Gospel Traditions: Feminist Celebrations.* Silver Spring, MD: WATERworks Press, 1989.

_____. *Liturgia: Un Jardin Compartido.* Silver Spring, MD: WATERworks Press, 1995.

_____. *Gathered at Sophia's Table.* Silver Spring, MD: WATERworks Press, 2001.

_____. *Peace Liturgies.* Silver Spring, MD: WATERworks Press, 2001.

Neu, Diann L., Tobie Hofman, Barbara Cullom, and Mindy Shapiro. *Miriam's Sisters Rejoice.* Silver Spring, MD: WATERworks Press, 1988.

Neu, Diann L., and Mary E. Hunt. *Women of Fire: A Pentecost Event.* Silver Spring, MD: WATERworks Press, 1990.

_____. *Women-Church Sourcebook.* Silver Spring, MD: WATERworks Press, 1993.

Neu, Diann L., and Ronnie Levin. *A Seder of the Sisters of Sarah: A Holy Thursday and Passover Seder*. Silver Spring, MD: WATERworks Press, 1986.

Neu, Diann L., Jessica Weissman, and Barbara Cullom. *Together at Freedom's Table*. Silver Spring, MD: WATERworks Press, 1991.

Orenstein, Rabbi Debora, ed. *Lifecycles: Jewish Women on Life Passages & Personal Milestones*. Woodstock, VT: Jewish Lights Publishing, 1994.

Richardson, Jan L. *Sacred Journeys: A Woman's Book of Daily Prayer*. Nashville: Upper Room Books, 1995.

Rienstra, Marchiene Vroon. *Swallow's Nest: A Feminist Reading of the Psalms*. Grand Rapids: William B. Eerdmans, 1992.

Roberts, Elizabeth, and Elias Amidon, eds. *Earth Prayers*. San Francisco: HarperSanFrancisco, 1991.

————. *Life Prayers*. San Francisco: HarperSanFrancisco, 1996.

————. *Prayers for a Thousand Years*. San Francisco: HarperSanFrancisco, 1999.

Rowthorn, Anne, ed. *Earth and All the Stars: Reconnecting with Nature through Hymns, Stories, Poems, and Prayers from the World's Great Religions and Cultures*. Novato, CA: New World Library, 2000.

Ruether, Rosemary Radford. *Women-Church: Theology and Practice*. San Francisco: Harper & Row, 1985.

Schaffran, Janet, and Pat Kozak. *More Than Words: Prayer and Ritual for Inclusive Communities*. Oak Park, IL: Meyer Stone Books, 1986.

Schmitt, Mary Kathleen Speegle. *Seasons of the Feminine Divine: Cycle B, Christian Feminist Prayers for the Liturgical Cycle*. New York: Crossroad, 1993.

————. *Seasons of the Feminine Divine: Cycle C, Christian Feminist Prayers for the Liturgical Cycle*. New York: Crossroad, 1994.

————. *Seasons of the Feminine Divine: Cycle A, Christian Feminist Prayers for the Liturgical Cycle*. New York: Crossroad, 1995.

Sears, Marge. *Life-Cycle Celebrations for Women*. Mystic, CT: Twenty-Third Publications, 1989.

Sewell, Marilyn, ed. *Cries of the Spirit*. Boston: Beacon Press, 1991.

————. *Claiming the Spirit Within*. Boston: Beacon Press, 1996.

Spiegel, Marcia Shon, and Deborah Lipton Kremsdorf. *Women Speak to God*. San Diego: Women's Intsitute for Continuing Jewish Education, 1987.

St. Hilda Community. *Women Included: A Book of Services and Prayers*. London: SPCK, 1991.

Stuart, Elizabeth, ed. *Daring to Speak Love's Name: A Gay and Lesbian Prayer Book*. London: Hamish Hamilton, 1992.

Swidler, Arlene, ed. *Sistercelebrations*. Philadelphia: Fortress Press, 1974.

Ward, Hannah, and Jennifer Wild, eds. *Human Rites: Worship Resources for an Age of Change*. London: Mowbray, 1995.

Ward, Hannah, Jennifer Wild, and Janet Morley, eds. *Celebrating Women*. London: SPCK, 1995.

Webster, Linda. *Womancircle Rituals: Celebrating Life, Sparking Connections*. Austin, TX: Women's Spirituality Group, First Unitarian Church, 1988.

Winter, Miriam Therese. *Woman Prayer, Woman Song: Resources for Ritual*. Oak Park, IL: Meyer Stone Books, 1987.

_____. *WomanWord: A Feminist Lectionary and Psalter. Women of the New Testament*. New York: Crossroad, 1990.

_____. *WomanWisdom: A Feminist Lectionary and Psalter. Women of the Hebrew Scriptures: Part One*. New York: Crossroad, 1991.

_____. *WomanWitness: A Feminist Lectionary and Psalter. Women of the Hebrew Scriptures: Part Two*. New York: Crossroad, 1992.

Women's Ordination Conference. *Liberating Liturgies*. Fairfax, VA: Women's Ordination Conference, 1989.

World Council of Churches. *Prayer & Poems, Songs & Stories: Ecumenical Decade 1988–1998*. Geneva, Switzerland: WCC Publications, 1988.

Women Musicians and Their Music

Duck, Ruth, and Michael G. Bausch, eds. *Everflowing Streams: Songs for Worship*. Pilgrim Press, 700 Prospect Avenue, Cleveland, OH 44115-1100. 1981. Book.

Friedman, Debbie. *And You Shall Be a Blessing*. Sounds Write Productions, Inc. 6685 Norman Lane, San Diego, CA 92120. 619-697-6120. www.soundswrite.com. 1988. Audiocassette.

Fulmer, Colleen. *Her Wings Unfurled*. Heartbeats, 20015 Detroit Road, Cleveland, OH 04416. 800-808-1991. 1989. Book, audiocassette.

_____. *Dancing Sophia's Circle*. Heartbeats. 1994. Book, audiocassette, compact disk.

_____. *Cry of Ramah*. Heartbeats. 1995. Book, audiocassette.

Getty, Adele. *O Great Spirit*. Spring Mill Music, P.O. Box 800, Boulder, CO 80306. 1989. Book, audiocassette, compact disk.

Huber, Jane Parker. *A Singing Faith*. Westminster John Knox Press, 100 Witherspoon Street, Louisville, KY 40202-1396. 1987. Book.

Kealoha, Anna. *Songs of the Earth, Music of the World*. Celestial Arts, P.O. Box 7327, Berkeley, CA 94707. 1989. Book.

Libana. *A Circle is Cast*. Libana, Inc., P. O. Box 400530, Cambridge, MA 02140. 800-997-7757. www.libana.com. libanainc@aol.com. 1986. Book, audiocassette.

_____. *Fire Within*. Libana. 1990. Book, audiocassette.

_____. *Night Passage*. Libana. 2000. Book, audiocassette, compact disk.

McDade, Carolyn. *Songs by Carolyn McDade*. Surtsey Publishing, 25 Wood-ridge Road, Orleans, MA, 02653-4806. 1982. Book.

_____. *Rain upon Dry Land*. Surtsey Publishing. 1984. Book, audiocassette.

_____. *This Touch Spun Web*. Surtsey Publishing. 1985. Book, audiocassette, compact disk.

_____. *The Best of Struggles*. Surtsey Publishing. 1989. Book, audiocassette, compact disk.

_____. *This Ancient Love*. Surtsey Publishing. 1990. Book, audiocassette, compact disk.

_____. *Songs for Congregational Singing*. Surtsey Publishing. 1991. Book.

Middleton, Julie Forest, ed. *Songs for Earthlings*. Emerald Earth Publishing, P.O. Box 4326, Philadelphia, PA 19118. 1998. Book.

Near, Holly. *Imagine My Surprise!* Hereford Music (ASCAP), P. O. Box 236, Ukiah, CA 95482. 510-286-7971. www.HollyNear.com. 1978. Audiocassette.

Pena, Donna. *Against the Grain—Contra La Corriente*. GIA Publications, Inc., 7404 S. Mason Avenue, Chicago, IL 60638. 1988. Audiocassette.

_____. *A New Heaven, A New Earth*, GIA Publications, Inc. 1993. Audiocassette.

Re-Imagining Community. *Bring the Feast: Songs from the Re-Imagining Community*. Pilgrim Press, 700 Prospect Avenue, Cleveland, OH 44115-1100. 1998. Book.

Sherman, Kathy. *Touch the Earth*. Sisters of St. Joseph. LaGrange, IL, 60525. 800-354-3504. www.ministryofthehearts.org. 1987. Audiocassette, compact disk.

_____. *Gather the Dreamers*. Sisters of St. Joseph. 1991. Audiocassette, compact disk.

_____. *Upon a Universe*. Sisters of St. Joseph. 1992. Audiocassette, compact disk.

_____. *Dance in the Dawn*. Sisters of St. Joseph. 1993. Audiocassette, compact disk.

_____. *Coming Home*. Sisters of St. Joseph. 1994. Book, audiocassette, compact disk.

Silvestro, Marsie. *Circling Free*. Moonsong Productions, 79 Mt. Pleasant Avenue, Glouchester, MA, 01930. 978-282-1655. 1983. Book, audiocassette, compact disk.

_____. *Crossing the Lines*. Moonsong Productions. 1987. Book, audiocassette, compact disk.

_____. *On the Other Side*. Moonsong Productions. 1993. Book, audiocassette, compact disk.

Sweet Honey in the Rock. *B'lieve I'll Run On . . . See What the End's Gonna Be.* Flying Fish Records, Inc., 1304 W. Schubert, Chicago, IL 60614. 1978. Book, audiocassette, compact disk.

————. *Good News.* Flying Fish Records 1981. Book, audiocassette, compact disk.

Ware, SL, Ann Patrick. *New Words for Old Hymns and Songs,* Women's Liturgy Group of New York City, c/o Claire S. Derway, 1120 Fifth Avenue, New York, NY 10128. 212-860-0980. 2000. Book.

Wendelborn, Betty. *Sing Green: Songs of the Mystics.* Pyramid Press, 29 King Edward Street, Mount Eden, Auckland 3, New Zealand. 1988. Book, audiocassette.

Winter, Miriam Theresa. *Woman Prayer, Woman Song.* Crossroad Publishing, 370 Lexington Avenue, New York, NY 10017. 1990. Book.

————. *Songlines: Hymns, Songs, Rounds and Refrains for Prayer and Praise.* Crossroad Publishing. 1996. Book.

Other Works of Interest

Adams, Carol, ed. *Ecofeminism and the Sacred.* New York: Continuum, 1993.

Allen, Paula Gunn. *The Sacred Hoop: Recovering the Feminine in American Indian Traditions.* Boston: Beacon Press, 1986.

————. *Grandmothers of the Light: A Medicine Woman's Sourcebook.* Boston: Beacon Press, 1991.

Amoah, Elizabeth, ed. *Where God Reigns.* Accra, Ghana: Circle of Concerned African Women Theologians, 1997.

Andrews, Lynn. *Teachings around the Sacred Wheel.* San Francisco: Harper & Row, 1990.

Aquino, Maria Pilar. *Our Cry for Life: Feminist Theology from Latin America.* Maryknoll, NY: Orbis Books, 1993.

Baker-Fletcher, Karen. *Sisters of Dust, Sisters of Spirit: Womanist Wordings on God and Creation.* Minneapolis: Fortress Press, 1998.

Berger, Teresa, ed. *Women's Ways of Worship: Gender Analysis and Liturgical History.* Collegeville, MN: Liturgical Press, 1999.

————. *Dissident Daughters: Feminist Liturgies in Global Context.* Louisville: Westminster John Knox Press, 2001.

Berry, Thomas, with Thomas Clarks. *Befriending the Earth: A Theology of Reconciliation between Humans and the Earth.* Mystic, CT: Twenty-Third Publications, 1991.

Beryl, Ingram. "Eco-justice Liturgies." In *Theology for Earth Community.* Edited by Dieter T. Hessel. Maryknoll, NY: Orbis Books, 1996.

Boff, Leonardo. *Ecology and Theology: A New Paradigm*. Maryknoll, NY: Orbis Books, 1995.

Braidotti, Rosi, Ewa Charkiewicz, Sabine Hausler, and Saskia Wieringa. *Women, the Environment and Sustainable Development*. London: Zed Books, 1994.

Brenneman, Walter L., and Mary G. Brenneman. *Crossing the Circle at the Holy Wells of Ireland*. Charlottesville, VA: University Press of Virginia, 1995.

Brenner, Athalya, ed. *A Feminist Companion to Genesis*. Sheffield, England: Sheffield Academic Press, 1993.

Broner, E. M. *Bringing Home the Light: A Jewish Woman's Handbook of Rituals*. San Francisco: Council Oak Books, 1999.

Budapest, Zsuzsanna E. *The Grandmother of Time*. San Francisco: Harper & Row, 1979.

Cameron, Anne. *Daughters of Copper Woman*. Vancouver: Press Gang Publishers, 1981.

Caron, Charlotte. *To Make and Make Again: Feminist Ritual Thealogy*. New York: Crossroad, 1993.

Carson, Rachel. *The Sense of Wonder*. San Francisco: HarperCollins, 1956.

Cassey, Helen Marie, and Amy Morgante. *Women's Views on the Earth Charter*. Boston: Boston Research Center for the 21st Century, 1997.

Christ, Carol. *The Rebirth of the Goddess: Finding Meaning in Feminist Spirituality*. Reading, MA: Addison-Wesley, 1997.

Chung Hyun-Kyung. *Struggle to Be the Sun Again: Introducing Asian Women's Theology*. Maryknoll, NY: Orbis Books, 1990.

Clifford, Anne M. "An Ecofeminist Proposal for Solidarity." In *In the Embrace of God: Feminist Approaches to Theological Anthropology*. Edited by Ann O'Hara Graff. Maryknoll, NY: Orbis Books, 1995.

Collins, Mary, and David Power, eds. *Blessing and Power*. Edinburgh, Scotland: T. and T. Clark, 1985.

Cooey, Paula, W. R. Eakin, and J. B. McDaniel, eds. *After Patriarchy: Feminist Transformations of the World Religions*. Maryknoll, NY: Orbis Books, 1991.

Cotner, June. *Animal Blessings: Prayers and Poems Celebrating Our Pets*. San Francisco: HarperSanFrancisco, 2000.

Diamond, Irene, and Gloria Fenman Orenstein, eds. *Reweaving the World: The Emergence of Ecofeminism*. San Francisco: Sierra Club Books, 1990.

Dietrich, Gabriele. *Reflections on the Women's Movements in India: Religion, Ecology and Development*. Delhi: Horizon India Books, 1992.

Doyle, Brendan, ed. *Meditations with Julian of Norwich*. Sante Fe, NM: Bear & Co., 1983.

Driver, Tom F. *Liberating Rites: Understanding the Transformative Power of Ritual*. Boulder, Co: Westview Press, 1998.

Duck, Ruth. *Finding Words for Worship: A Guide for Leaders.* Louisville: Westminster John Knox Press, 1995.

Elkins, Heather Murray. *Worshiping Women: Re-forming God's People for Praise.* Nashville: Abingdon Press, 1994.

Fabella, Virginia M. M., and Mercy Amba Oduyoye. *With Passion and Compassion: Third World Women Doing Theology.* Maryknoll, NY: Orbis Books, 1988.

Fabella, Virginia M. M., and Sun Ai Lee Park. *We Dare to Dream: Doing Theology as Asian Women.* Seoul, Korea: The Asian Women's Resource Center.

Gebara, Ivone. *Longing for Running Water: Ecofeminism and Liberation.* Minneapolis: Fortress Press, 1999.

———. "Ecofeminismo holistico," *Revista Con-spirando,* 4 (June 1993), 5–8.

———. *Intuiciones Ecofeministas.* Montevideo, Uruguay: Doble clic, 1998.

Gimbutas, Marija. *The Language of the Goddess.* San Francisco: Harper & Row, 1989.

Gottlieb, Roger, ed. *This Sacred Earth: Religion, Nature, Environment.* New York and London: Routledge, 1996.

Griffin, Susan. *Woman and Nature: The Roaring Inside Her.* New York: Harper & Row, 1978.

Habel, Norman C., ed. *Readings from the Perspective of Earth.* Cleveland, OH: Pilgrim Press, 2000.

Habel, Norman C., and Shirley Wurst, eds. *The Earth Story in Genesis.* Cleveland, OH: Pilgrim Press, 2000.

Hallman, David, ed. *Ecotheology: Voices from South and North.* Maryknoll, NY: Orbis Books, 1994.

———. *Spiritual Values for Earth Community.* Geneva, Switzerland: WCC Publications, 2000.

Hessel, Dieter T. *Theology for Earth Community.* Maryknoll, NY: Orbis Books, 1996.

Hessel, Dieter T., and Larry Rasmussen, eds. *Earth Habitat: Eco-justice and the Church's Response.* Minneapolis: Fortress Press, 2001.

Hessel, Dieter T., and Rosemary Radford Ruether. *Christianity and Ecology: Seeking the Well-Being of Earth and Humans.* Cambridge, MA: Harvard University Press, 2000.

Hinshaw, Annette. *Earthtime, Moontime: Rediscovering the Sacred Lunar Year.* St. Paul: Llewellyn Publications, 1999.

Imber-Black, Evan, and Janine Roberts. *Rituals for Our Times.* New York: HarperCollins, 1992.

Isasi-Diaz, Ada Maria. *Mujerista Theology.* Maryknoll, NY: Orbis Books, 1996.

Johnson, Elisabeth. *Women, Earth, and Creator Spirit.* New York: Paulist Press, 1993.

Joranson, Philip N. *Cry of the Environment.* Sante Fe: Bear & Co., 1984.

Journal of Asian Women's Resource Centre and Theology. In *God's Image: Women, Ecology and Eco-Feminism.* Kuala Lumpur, Malaysia: Asian Women's Resource Centre for Culture and Theology. 18, no. 3 (September 2000).

Kannyoro, Musimbi R. A., and Nyambura J. Njoroge, eds. *Groaning in Faith: African Women in the Household of God.* Nairobi, Kenya: Acton Publishers, 1996.

Kelly, Petra. *Thinking Green!* Berkeley: Parallax Press, 1994.

King, Ursula, ed. *Feminist Theology from the Third World: A Reader.* Maryknoll, NY: Orbis Books, 1994.

Knie, Ute, and Herta Leistner. *Lass horen deine Stimme: Werkstattbuch Feministische Liturgie.* Guterslo: Gutersloher Verlagshaus, 1999.

Kwok, Pui-lan. "Mending of Creation: Women, Nature and Eschatological Hope." In *Liberating Eschatology: Essays in Honor of Letty M. Russell.* Edited by Margaret A. Farley and Serene Jones. Louisville: Westminster John Knox Press, 1999.

_____. *Introducing Asian Feminist Theology.* Cleveland, OH: Pilgrim Press, 2000.

Lear, Linda, ed. *Lost Woods: The Discovered Writing of Rachel Carson.* Boston: Beacon Press, 1998.

Luckett, Rosemary. *Prayer Trees.* Manassas, VA: Second River Studio, 1998.

Macey, Joanna, and Molly Young Brown. *Coming Back to Life: Practices to Reconnect Our Lives, Our World.* Philadelphia: New Society Publishers, 1998.

MacKinnon, Mary Heather. *Readings in Ecology and Feminist Theology.* Kansas City, MO: Sheed & Ward, 1995.

Mananzan, Mary John, Mercy Amba Oduyoye, Elsa Tamez, J. Shannon Clarkson, Mary C. Grey, and Letty M. Russell, eds. *Women Resisting Violence.* Maryknoll, NY: Orbis Books, 1996.

Matthews, Caitlin. *The Blessing Seed: A Creation Myth for the New Millennium.* Bath, England: Barefoot Books, 1998.

McCarthy, Scott. *Celebrating the Earth: An Earth-Centered Theology of Worship with Blessings, Prayers, and Rituals.* San Jose, CA: Resource Publications, 1987.

McCoy, Edain. *Celtic Women's Spirituality.* St Paul: Llewellyn, 1998.

McFague, Sallie. *The Body of God: An Ecological Theology.* Minneapolis: Fortress Press, 1993.

_____. *Super, Natural Christians: How We Should Love Nature.* Minneapolis: Fortress Press, 1997.

_____. *Life Abundant: Rethinking Theology and Economy for a Planet in Peril.* Minneapolis: Fortress Press, 2001.

Merchant, Carolyn. *The Death of Nature: Women, Ecology and the Scientific Revolution.* San Francisco: Harper & Row, 1980.

_____. *Radical Ecology: The Search for a Livable World.* New York: Routledge, 1992.

Miles, Maria, and Vandana Shiva. *Ecofeminism.* Halifax, NS: Fernwood Publications; Atlantic Highlands, NJ: Zed Books, 1993.

Moorey, Teresa, and Jane Brideson. *Wheel of the Year: Myth and Magic through the Seasons.* London: Bath Press, 1997.

Morrison, Dorothy. *Yule: A Celebration of Light and Warmth.* St. Paul: Llewellyn, 2000.

Mueller-Fahrenholz, Geiko. *God's Spirit: Transforming a World in Crisis.* New York: Continuum, 1995.

Newsom, Carol A., and Sharon H. Ringe, eds. *Women's Bible Commentary.* Louisville: Westminster John Knox Press, 1998.

Niethammer, Carolyn. *Daughters of the Earth: The Lives and Legends of American Indian Women.* New York: Collier Books, 1977.

Oduyoye, Mercy Amba. *Daughters of Anowa: African Women and Patriarchy.* Maryknoll, NY: Orbis Books, 1995.

Oduyoye, Mercy Amba, and Musimbi Kanyoro. *The Will to Rise: Women, Tradition and the Church in Africa.* Maryknoll, NY: Orbis Books, 1992.

Pennick, Nigel. *Celtic Sacred Landscapes.* London, England: Thames and Hudson, 1996.

Piercy, Marge. *The Moon Is Always Female.* New York: Alfred A. Knopf, 1980.

Plant, Judith. *Healing the Wounds: The Promise of Ecofeminism.* Philadelphia: New Society Publishers, 1989.

Primavesi, Anne. *From Apocalypse to Genesis: Ecology, Feminism and Christianity.* Minneapolis: Fortress Press, 1991.

Procter-Smith, Marjorie. *In Her Own Rite: Constructing Feminist Liturgical Tradition.* Nashville: Abingdon Press, 1990.

_____. *Praying with Our Eyes Open: Engendering Feminist Liturgical Prayer.* Nashville: Abingdon Press, 1995.

Qoyawayma, Polingaysi. *No Turning Back.* As told to Vada F. Carlson. Albuquerque, NM: University of New Mexico Press, 1964.

Rae, Eleanor. *Created in Her Image.* New York: Crossroad, 1990.

_____. *Women, the Earth, the Divine.* Maryknoll, NY: Orbis Books, 1994.

Ress, Mary Judith, Ute Siebert-Cuadra, and Lene Siorup, eds. *Del Cielo a la Tierra: Una Antolotia de Teologia Feminista.* Santiago, Chile: Sello Azul, 1994.

Ress, Judy. "The Ecofeminist Paradigm" (mimeo). Santiago, Chile, 1993.

Rich, Adrienne. *The Dream of a Common Language: Poems 1974–1977.* New York: W. W. Norton, 1978.

Roberts, Wendy. *Celebrating Her: Feminist Ritualizing Comes of Age.* Cleveland, OH: Pilgrim Press, 1998.

Rossato, Veronica. "Feminismo y Ecologia." *Mujer/Fempress*, no. 93 (1989).

————. "Una Vision Ecofeminista del Manejo de los Recuros Naturales," *Mujer/Fempress*, no. 115 (1991).

Ruether, Rosemary Radford. *New Women, New Earth: Sexist Ideologies and Human Liberation.* New York: Seabury Press, 1975.

————. *Sexism and God-Talk: Toward a Feminist Theology.* Boston: Beacon Press, 1983.

————. *Women-Church: Theology and Practice.* San Francisco: Harper & Row, 1985.

————. *Gaia and God: An Ecofeminist Theology of Earth Healing.* San Francisco: Harper & Row, 1992.

————, ed. *Women Healing Earth: Third World Women on Ecology, Feminism and Religion.* Maryknoll, NY: Orbis Books, 1996.

Ruether, Rosemary, and Dieter Hessel, eds. *Christianity and Ecology.* Cambridge, MA: Harvard University Press, 2000.

Russell, Letty M. *Church in the Round: Feminist Interpretation of the Church.* Louisville: Westminster John Knox Press, 1993.

Russell, Letty M., and Shannon Clarkson, eds. *Dictionary of Feminist Theologies.* Louisville: Westminster John Knox Press, 1996.

Sarton, May. *Collected Poems (1930–1973).* New York: W. W. Norton, 1974.

Schüssler Fiorenza, Elisabeth. *In Memory of Her: A Feminist Theological Reconstruction of Christian Origins.* Reprint. New York: Crossroad, 1983/1994.

————. *But She Said: Feminist Practices of Biblical Interpretation.* Boston: Beacon Press, 1992.

————. *Discipleship of Equals: A Critical Feminist Ekklesialogy of Liberation.* New York: Crossroad, 1993.

Sheehan, Kathryn, and Mary Waidner. *Earth Child 2000: Earth Science for Young Children, Games, Stories, Activities, and Experiments.* Tulsa/San Francisco: Council Oak Books, 1998.

Shiva, Vandana. *Staying Alive: Women, Ecology and Development.* Delhi, India: Kali for Women, 1988.

Sjoo, Monica, and Barbara Mor. *The Great Cosmic Mother: Rediscovering the Religion of the Earth.* San Francisco: Harper & Row, 1987.

Skinner, John, trans. and ed. *Revelation of Love.* New York: Doubleday, 1996.

Spretnak, Charlene. *The Politics of Women's Spirituality.* New York: Anchor Press, 1982.

Starck, Marcia. *Earth Mother Astrology.* St. Paul: Llewellyn, 1989.

Starhawk. *The Spiral Dance: A Rebirth of the Ancient Religion of the Great Goddess.* 2nd ed. San Francisco: Harper & Row, 1989.

Stepanich, Kisma K. *The Gaia Tradition.* St. Paul: Llewellyn, 1991.

Suzuki, David, with Amanda McConnell. *The Sacred Balance: Rediscovering Our Place in Nature.* New South Wales, Australia: Allen and Unwin, 1997.

Swimme, Brian. *The Universe Is a Green Dragon: a Cosmic Creation Story.* Santa Fe, NM: Bear & Co., 1984.

_____. *The Hidden Heart of the Cosmos: Humanity and the New Story.* Maryknoll, NY: Orbis Books, 1996.

Swimme, Brian, and Thomas Berry. *The Universe Story.* San Francisco: HarperSanFrancisco, 1992.

Trapassso, Rosa Domingo. "Ecofeminismo: revisando nuestra conexion con la naturaleza," *Con-spirando* 4 (June 1993).

_____. *Ecologia: Una vision global y transformadora.* Lima: Circulo de Feministas Cristianas Talitha Cumi, no. 24 (1993).

Uhlein, Gabriele, ed. *Meditations with Hildegard of Bingen.* Santa Fe, NM: Bear & Co., 1982.

Walker, Alice. *In Search of Our Mothers' Gardens: Womanist Prose.* New York: Harcourt Brace Jovanovich, 1983.

_____. *Living By the Word.* New York: Harcourt Brace Jovanovich, 1988.

_____. *Temple of My Familiar.* New York: Simon and Schuster, 1989.

Walton, Janet R. *Feminist Liturgy: A Matter of Justice.* Collegeville, MN: Liturgical Press, 2000.

Ward, Barbara, and Rene Dubos. *Only One Earth: The Care and Maintenance of a Small Planet.* New York: W. W. Norton, 1972.

Women, Ecology and Eco-feminism issue of *In God's Image.* Seoul, Korea: Journal of Asian Women's Resource Centre for Culture and Theology, 19, no. 3 (September 2000).

Wood, Catherine. "Ritual of the Elements." In *Women, Ecology and Eco-feminism* issue of *In God's Image.* Seoul, Korea: Journal of Asian Women's Resource Centre for Culture and Theology, 19, no. 3 (September 2000), 48–52.

INDEX